'Kris Østergaard does an amazing job highlighting and defining the key issues preventing established companies from transforming: the individual immune system, the societal immune system, and the organizational immune system. His book is a must read if you are hoping to be the disruptor and not the disrupted in this age of unicorns.'

Salim Ismail, bestselling author of Exponential Organizations

'*Transforming Legacy Organizations* is a great manual for any company looking to transform itself in the face of accelerating technology and fierce competition. Both a fun read and incredibly informative. A welcome addition to the innovation canon!'

Steven Kotler, New York Times bestselling author of Bold,
Abundance, and The Rise of Superman

'Innovation is not just for the young and digital. As Kris Østergaard makes clear, legacy organizations can also – must also! – innovate to create economic value now and into the future. Don't let the size of this book fool you, for it provides a road map any company can follow to overcome the immune systems that stifle change and innovation. Follow this path in transforming your legacy organization to snatch victory from the jaws of disruption.'

B. Joseph Pine II, bestselling co-author of The
Experience Economy

'While innovation is increasingly important, the term innovation has been so overused that practitioners are left feeling confused and unsure what to do next . . . *Transforming Legacy Organizations* is the antidote to this innovation abstraction. This book is practical, helpful, and accessible. I highly recommend it.'

Kyle Nel, bestselling author of Leading Transformation, *former Executive Director for Lowe's Innovation Labs*

'After 10 years of helping companies disrupt themselves, we are also finding how hard it is to do it ourselves at Singularity University. *Transforming Legacy Organizations* outlines many of the barriers we created in our journey to get here and how to break through them in order to continue to be at the leading edge of exponential change and technological disruption.'

Rob Nail, CEO & Associate Founder of Singularity University

TRANSFORMING LEGACY ORGANIZATIONS

TRANSFORMING LEGACY ORGANIZATIONS

TURN YOUR ESTABLISHED BUSINESS INTO AN INNOVATION CHAMPION TO WIN THE FUTURE

KRIS ØSTERGAARD

WILEY

Registered office
John Wiley & Sons Ltd, The Atrium, Southern Gate, Chichester, West Sussex, PO19 8SQ, United Kingdom

For details of our global editorial offices, for customer services and for information about how to apply for permission to reuse the copyright material in this book please see our website at www.wiley.com.

Library of Congress Cataloging-in-Publication Data

Names: Østergaard, Kris, 1973- author.
Title: Transforming legacy organizations : turn your established business
    into an innovation champion to win the future / Kris Østergaard.
Description: Chichester, West Sussex, United Kingdom : John Wiley & Sons,
    [2019] | Includes bibliographical references and index. |
    Identifiers: LCCN 2019008178 (print) | LCCN 2019011558 (ebook) | ISBN
    9781119583547 (Adobe PDF) | ISBN 9781119583561 (ePub) | ISBN 9781119583509
    (hardback)
Subjects: LCSH: Technological innovations—Management. | New products. |
    Organizational change. | Strategic planning.
Classification: LCC HD45 (ebook) | LCC HD45 .O28 2019 (print) | DDC
    658.4/063—dc23
LC record available at https://lccn.loc.gov/2019008178

Cover Design: Wiley
Cover Image: © BombSymbols/Shutterstock

Set in 12/18pt MinionPro by SPi Global, Chennai, India

Printed in Great Britain by TJ International Ltd, Padstow, Cornwall, UK

10 9 8 7 6 5 4 3 2 1

Dedicated to the most important ones:
Laila, Zoey, Louise, Emilie and Izabella.

Most of our assumptions have outlived their uselessness.

Marshall McLuhan

CONTENTS

INTRODUCTION

We live in the age of the entrepreneurs. New startups seem to appear out of nowhere and challenge not only established companies, but entire industries. Where unicorns were once mythical creatures, the word unicorn now refers to the startups that have a value of at least one billion dollars, and, at the time of writing this, there are more than 260 of them worldwide.[1] In 2018 alone, 53 unicorns were added to the list. You have probably never heard of the most valuable one. It's called ByteDance and it comes from China; it is a kind of a mix between Google and Facebook, and it is valued at $75 billion.[2] The fastest unicorn, the software company Uptake, took only 236 days to reach billion-dollar status from their first invested dollar.[3] And the Nordic countries, where I come from, actually make up the largest unicorn region in the world, after Silicon Valley, in large part thanks to Stockholm which represents success stories like Spotify, Klarna, and King.[4]

Not long ago, young people dreamed of becoming doctors and lawyers. Today, an increasing number of youths are dreaming of becoming entrepreneurs and creating companies that can change the world – just like the new heroes Elon Musk (Tesla), Larry Page (Google) or Jeff Bezos (Amazon). The whole unicorn wave is so great that it has moved into the mass market. So if you have children between the ages of 8–10 who want teddy bears, suits and clothes from H&M with unicorns on them, their preferences are examples of how the startup wave has spread into our everyday life. The established organizations, those of a certain size and age (sometimes called legacy organizations) are becoming stressed about entrepreneurs' success and can be quoted as saying that their greatest fear is not their closest major competitors; rather, they fear the startups which, although they live in metaphorical garages and have hardly taken off, have an innovation power that established organizations could only dream of possessing.

But no matter how good things go for the innovative startups, how many new success stories we hear, and how much space they take up in the media, there's both good and bad news in terms of established companies' innovation power. The bad news is that innovation is much more difficult in established organizations than it is in startups. The most important job for a startup is to focus on its (probably one) product, and to subsequently scale-up. The established organizations have to entertain many more considerations with their complicated product portfolios and business structures. The good news, however, is that nobody is more likely to succeed in their innovation efforts than established organizations. Because, unlike startups, established organizations have all the resources. They have money, customers, data, employees, suppliers, partners, and infrastructure, which put them in a far better position to transform new ideas into concrete value-creating, successful services. Startups have very few of these tools.

Of all startups, 70% fail within approximately 20 months of their first venture round[5] and there is an overall greater risk of being hit by lightning (about 1: 700,000) than there is of creating a unicorn. So when the big, established players are terrified of entrepreneurs, it's because they have not figured out how they can beat the startup in its own game: innovation.

This book's thesis is that established organizations have every opportunity to become the victors of the future. But to achieve this, they need to create a future-proof innovation design or, in other words, to put the right strategies in place and to develop the necessary processes to drive internal and external organizational innovation. The method for this is not to copy startups, because innovation in a startup is completely different from innovation in an established organization. However, if you look carefully at what the big, established players are doing right in terms of innovation, you can identify a number of patterns that point towards what the right innovation design looks like, i.e. the design that can create value across industries. In the following, I will be clarifying these patterns.

I have identified the most important of these patterns in the work and research I've done over the past 20 years in both established businesses and startups across the globe, in hundreds of case analyses from world leading companies, in global market analyses, in basic research on innovation, culture, and change processes, as well as through interviews with key figures from a number of leading international companies. In my research, I have not met one singular established organization that has figured it all out, and which could therefore serve as an example from which to simply copy best practices. Some of the companies that get the closest to this level are organizations like Amazon, Google, and Apple, which are sometimes erroneously referred to as startups, even though each of these companies has been around for more than 20 years – Apple has even been around for 40. They are characterized by having reinvented themselves several times, a crucial characteristic of the established organizations that we return to. But there is also much to learn from companies with an even longer history: the Danish water pump manufacturer Grundfos, the North American Fortune 40 DIY chain Lowe's, the leading logistics company Maersk, the US production giant GE, and Japan's no. 1 airline ANA.

Before we look into what these companies are doing well, and what other large and less-established organizations could learn from, we need to define a few things. What do I really mean when I write 'innovation' and 'innovation design'? Innovation is the act of creating something new and having it materialize. It could, for example, involve creating direct market-oriented products or services, but it could also be the creation of new internal processes or production methods. Innovation is not limited to market-oriented initiatives, and therefore innovation is not something that is only relevant to product development teams; rather, it is relevant to the entire organization.

However, simply thinking fresh and having ideas is not enough. The ideas should be realizable. That is to say, they must result in specific products, services, business models, or processes. Too many times, you see organizations which set up so-called innovation initiatives, but do not follow through, which results in the experience that you, most likely, know well: you get many great ideas, but have a hard time turning them into concrete value. The ideas do not materialize because the organization lacks a well-functioning innovation design. According to the *Oxford Dictionary*, design is defined as 'the art or the action of inventing and creating a plan or sketch of something before executing on it'.[6] And innovation design is exactly that: A plan for how to shape your innovations, so that you don't leave its success to chance. With an innovation design, you actually have a plan, a design, for how to go from idea to development to rollout. Established organizations are often world champions in planning when it comes to traditional product development, but when it comes to innovation in a modern age, they need new rules of engagement. As will be evident in the book, many organizations commit the mistake of engaging in innovation as if it were a homogeneous thing that should be approached in the same way every time, regardless of its purpose. But innovation in established organizations must actually be divided into three different tracks: optimizing, augmenting, and mutating innovation. All three are important. There is no one singular type of innovation that is better than others. And to complicate matters further, organizations must execute all three types of innovation at the same time.

The first track is optimizing innovation. This type of innovation is the majority of what established organizations already do today. And they must continue doing so. Optimizing innovation is, simply put, the extra blade on the razor. When Gillette launches a new razor that has not just three, but four blades, thus ensuring an even better, closer, and more comfortable shave, only to announce one or two years later that they are now launching a razor that has not only four, but five blades – so you get an even better, closer, and more comfortable shave – that is optimizing innovation. This is where the established player reigns. No startup with so much as a modicum of sense would even try to beat the established company in that type of innovation. Continuous optimization of current things, both on the operational aspect and customer aspect, is good and important. In the short term. It pays the rent. But it's far from being enough if you want to continue being a leader even just 3–5 years from now, because there are limits to how many blades a razor needs, and each additional blade generates a bit less value than the previous one.

Therefore, the established players must also focus on the second track: augmenting innovation. If you look at the digital transformation projects that more and more organizations are initiating, they can typically be characterized as augmenting innovation. In the first instance, it is about upgrading the organizations and their core services and processes from analogue to digital. Or, if you're born digital, you've probably had to work on augmentation to become 'mobile first'. Perhaps you have even entered the next augmenting phase, which involves implementing artificial intelligence at the heart of your organization. To become 'AI first'. These problems that need solving are not small matters. They require great technological advancements. And it's difficult. But the technology component may, in fact, be a minor part of the task. When it comes to augmenting innovation, the biggest challenge is probably culture. Because it is only if the established organizations manage to transform their cultures from status quo cultures, i.e. cultures where there is a preference to maintain things as they are, into cultures full of incremental innovators who thrive in constant change (within certain limits) that they will have a shot at success.

To achieve success with augmenting innovation and to create the right culture, an organization needs to thoroughly understand its immune systems. That is to say, it knows the barriers that inhibit its innovative power in the form of the individual, organizational, and societal immune systems, which can either impede or support innovation. Augmenting innovation is crucial if you want success in the medium term.

After optimizing and augmenting innovation, an established organization needs to relate to the long term and innovate in the track that creates the potential for mutating innovation. The business that maintains, or exceeds, its level of success 10, 20, 30 years from now will have mutated and will look significantly different than it does today. It will have changed form. Whatever is currently the core of the company making up the majority of the top and bottom lines will not remain the same in the long run. Mutating innovation requires a bold focus on experimenting with that which is not currently understood. You have to work in a different way than when you're designing for augmenting innovation, because there is a big difference in whether you innovate to upgrade the core, as is done with augmenting innovation, or you're challenging the core as you do with mutating innovation.

The book is divided into three parts, each exploring how to tackle this task. The first part, 'Sharpen the Axe', focuses on how best to prepare for innovation as an established organization. There are a number of questions you should ask yourself. Questions that you have probably asked yourself before, but that you should revisit with fresh eyes. Because the answers to questions about which industry one is in, who one's competitors are, what drives the customers, and what the purpose of it all really is, are not as obvious as they once were. But it is crucial that you conduct your analyses and thoroughly explore those questions so that you can implement the right strategy, create the right innovation design, and put the right initiatives in motion.

The second part of the book focuses on the immune systems, the mechanisms, that protect the organizations and which operate around the clock to keep them healthy and stable, just as the body's immune system operates to keep the body healthy and stable. In a rapidly changing world, many of these defence mechanisms are no longer appropriate and therefore risk weakening organizations' innovation power. When talking about organizations' immune systems, there is a clear tendency to simply point out people's unwillingness to change. But this answer is too simplistic and sloppy. As we will see, there is not only an individual, but also organizational and societal immune systems that all organizations must understand and design their innovation efforts by.

In part three, we ultimately dive into the three different innovation tracks that organizations must master. We won't spend much time on optimizing innovation here, because the established organizations are already masters at this, and it is the area which works on the short-term horizon. However, we will be heavily examining augmenting innovation and exploring which tools are available for successfully upgrading the core of the organization and, not least, how to use cultural hacks to develop its culture in the desired direction, as a strong innovation culture is crucial to its success. Finally, we focus on the most experimental part where organizations work with mutating innovation and challenge their own core to explore which organization they should become in the long term.

When diving into a field and exploring it more closely, it is always revealed to have depths and nuances so numerous that the art of limitation becomes crucial. Each of the chapters in this book deserves a book of its own. And elements in each of the book chapters have had books written about themselves in different ways. But time is precious. It is perhaps our most precious resource, because once you have given your time to an activity, you cannot get it back. Therefore, the intention here has been to write an easy-to-read book that provides a relatively quick overview of how established organizations should pursue innovation to create their future success. I personally love thin books. Books that I can read quickly, and which enable me to get an overview and draw value that relates to my specific needs. Then I can decide which elements of the book deserve my continued attention and which ones I will delve deeper into. Some of the focus areas of the book will, of course, be known to some readers. That's good. You can read through those parts more easily. Some of the sections will contain new material, at which point there is good reason to read the text more thoroughly. Some of the new material may even give so much food for thought that the reader wishes to explore further literature to obtain an even deeper understanding. Therefore, I have included an extensive bibliography with the background material that inspired me and helped create the foundation for this book.

Innovation is one of the things that established organizations talk most about, but also one of the things that they have the hardest time succeeding with. I hope this book will help to show how legacy organizations can innovate to become the champions of the future.

Kris Østergaard
Copenhagen
December 2018

NOTES

1. www.cbinsights.com/research/unicorn-startup-market-map.
2. https://exponentialview.us15.list-manage.com/track/click?u=eee7b8043
   119f98544067854b&id=8654d2b47f&e=e88e438a60.
3. https://officechai.com/startups/fastest-unicorn-startups.
4. www.weforum.org/agenda/2017/10/why-does-sweden-produce-so-
   many-startups.
5. CB insights Feb 27 2018.
6. https://en.oxforddictionaries.com/definition/design.

PART I

SHARPEN THE AXE

Give me six hours to chop down a tree and I will spend the first four sharpening the axe.

Abraham Lincoln

CHAPTER 1

FROM INNOVATION THEATRE TO INNOVATION CULTURE

Have you ever heard of a management team that goes to Silicon Valley to observe the natives in their natural habitats and decode their success strategies? Or maybe you've heard of big organizations that have invited a number of students to a hackathon, where they were going to disrupt the core product over the course of 24 hours, with the help of a large amount of (probably bad) data, pizzas, coffee, and Red Bull. Perhaps you have even encountered companies that have invested in an accelerator programme where they follow a group of startups over a few months in the hope of reaching the achievements that the core organization itself struggles with. There is nothing wrong as such with the aforesaid initiatives, even though I am describing them with some irony. I use these initiatives myself, and I sometimes find them to be extremely valuable. However, there is a great risk that the initiatives do not create the value that organizations want and need. And there is a great risk that they give organizations a false sense of security. For far too often, experience expeditions, hackathons, and accelerator programmes end up being singular events that do not materialize into anything of real value. They end up becoming innovation theatre rather than creating innovation culture. The companies' innovation efforts wind up not being ambitious enough, and management does not incorporate the initiatives in their corporate strategies because they do not fully understand how huge the implications of accelerating technological development are on their organizations' need to innovate.

Where the world was once local and linear, and we humans got up and went to bed with the sun's rising and falling, moved within a demarcated geographical area, and interacted with a rather limited number of other people, reality looks different today. The world is no longer local and linear. It is global and exponential, thanks to the technological achievements that have largely been sustained by Moore's law.[1] This law, which is not a law of nature but an observation, is named after Gordon

Moore, co-founder of the computer chip manufacturer Intel. More than 50 years ago, he observed that there was a potential for computer power to double roughly every two years by placing more transistors in the microchips that give computers their computing power. The doublings that he pointed out were in fact what are called price and performance doublings, i.e. the amount of attainable processing power per $1000. These doublings have evolved to be exceedingly stable and have been the foundation of the development of computing power for more than 50 years and, thus, also the basis for the digitization we see in our businesses and societies, and the fantastic developments within networks, sensors, artificial intelligence, robotics, 3D printing, digital biology, and a whole host of other technologies. It can be hard to understand how significant the development is and how strong it really is. But here are a few examples that illustrate the pace.

In Alphabet's (Google's parent company) annual Founders' Letter in April 2018, Alphabet co-founder Sergey Brin described just how extreme price and performance development has been since Google's first year. In Google's first year of existence, the Pentium II processor they used to run their search engine had a performance of approximately 100 million so-called floating point operations per second. Today, it has 20 billion. That's an increase by factor of 200,000.[2] But, as he also wrote, even this amazing development would mean nothing if they or others succeed in quantum computing experiments, which are receiving billion-dollar investments from Google as well as Microsoft, Facebook, Amazon, Alibaba, Tencent, and Softbank, just to name a few, along with major research efforts around the world, and even in Copenhagen, my own backyard, in the last few years. Development is also rapidly accelerating in artificial intelligence. According to the non-profit research institution Open AI, which researches artificial intelligence and was founded by Tesla's CEO Elon Musk and Sam Altman of Y Combinator (the world's most successful accelerator), the amount of compute for executing the biggest artificial intelligence training programs is doubling every 3.5 months (for comparison, Moore's law dictates a price-performance doubling time of about 18 months).[3] Thus, larger and larger datasets can be used to train artificial intelligences, which is crucial for their learning. It is, for example, this method which was used to train Alpha Go, the artificial intelligence that in 2017 beat the world's best Go player in this complicated game.[4]

The food producer Impossible Foods produces plant-based burgers that look like meat, taste like meat and bleed like meat, even though the burgers are 100% plant-based. The burgers behave like meat because the producer has developed a method of simulating the meat experience by adding heme, a component of an oxygen-bearing molecule that is also found in blood, to the plant material, thereby recreating the meat-like experience.

In 2016, Impossible Foods sold their burgers in around 200 American restaurants. In 2018, they began to produce over 500,000 kilograms of plant-based 'meat' mince in their new factory, thus truly preparing themselves to offer their products to the wider market,[5] which is increasingly open to a future where the cow itself gets disrupted, and meat no longer needs to be on the menu, as long as the meat experience is still possible.

In 2018, the first self-driving taxis were piloted on specified routes in selected cities in the United States (though still with a human controller for safety, and not without accidents and problems) and overall, the self-driving car manufacturer Waymo has now test-driven more than 16 million kilometres on the road,[6] and drives an additional 16 million virtual kilometres a day in a virtual world, a so-called digital twin that the company created to conduct more thorough testing.[7] Peter Thiel, investor and co-founder of payment solution PayPal and the data company Palantir, is known for the quote 'We were promised flying cars, instead we got 140 characters' (i.e. Twitter) in a critique of how little innovation tech companies have created. But this quote is about to be put to shame, as Dubai is playing with autonomous flying taxis and claims that they will be put into operation shortly. The latest virtual reality glasses from the manufacturer Oculus, launched in May 2018, do not need to be connected to a PC, inserted into a smartphone, or connected to headphones, like other models on the market. And they already cost only a quarter of what Oculus's own products did in 2017,[8] which means that the price level is about to hit a point where virtual reality glasses could actually become available to a broader target group.

The CRISPR-Cas9 genome editing technology was developed in 2012. It can, simply put, be compared to the cut-and-paste feature in a Word document, with the slight difference that CRISPR-Cas9 cuts and pastes DNA, the building blocks of life. We've been able to edit genes for more than 30 years, but precision, time, and pricing have been huge obstacles, and CRISPR seems to be the technology that radically changes this, thus paving the way for, among other things, rendering the world's biggest killer malaria mosquitoes harmless,[9] improving food resistance to disease and decay,[10] storing data in DNA,[11] bringing extinct animal species like mammoths back into the world,[12] and, not least, curing cancer.[13] Much of this sounds like science fiction, but it's scientific fact[14] and it is in the process of radically changing the world as we know it.

As a modern person, you would need to be walking around with blinkers to be completely unaware of even one of the developments that I have briefly described here. Nevertheless, only a minority of organizations possess sufficiently broad and deep knowledge about these developments, and many do not take them seriously enough. In fact, established organizations tend to do one of two things. Either they are dismissive of whatever is new and different, because these things are almost by definition difficult to fit into existing strategies. That is to say, that as a food producer, for instance, you look at Impossible Foods, which produces plant-based burgers, and say 'It's niche', 'It will never amount into anything', or 'It has nothing to do with us, we produce meat', while not realizing that consumers are increasingly open to meat alternatives, as long as they don't have to give up the meat experience . Alternatively, organizations recognize, on some level, that they should explore new things, but they don't do it thoroughly, ambitiously, and strategically enough. That's when they take the trip to Silicon Valley, or conduct a hackathon, or join an accelerator programme, all of which can be good and value-creating tools. But if you have not put forward a strategy for the future, these otherwise excellent initiatives end up becoming isolated events, a kind of innovation theatre, where you say and do some of the right things, but do not convert any of them into a strong innovation culture. Let's, therefore, look at the questions that you must ask or re-ask yourself to lay the foundation for the right strategy and the right innovation design.

NOTES

1. www.intel.com/content/www/us/en/history/museum-gordon-moore-law.html.
2. https://abc.xyz/investor/founders-letters/2017/index.html.
3. https://blog.openai.com/ai-and-compute.

4. https://deepmind.com/research/alphago.
5. https://techcrunch.com/2018/04/03/wheres-the-beef-for-impossible-foods-its-in-boosting-burger-sales-and-raising-hundreds-of-millions.
6. https://exponentialview.us15.list-manage.com/track/click?u=eee7b804 3119f98544067854b&id=ec15fe0e61&e=e88e438a60.
7. www.technologyreview.com/s/612251/waymos-cars-drive-10-million-miles-a-day-in-a-perilous-virtual-world.
8. https://arstechnica.com/gaming/2017/07/oculus-cuts-rift-price-for-second-time-this-year-now-399-with-touch/.
9. www.wired.com/story/heres-the-plan-to-end-malaria-with-crispr-edited-mosquitoes.
10. www.nature.com/news/gene-edited-crispr-mushroom-escapes-us-regulation-1.19754.
11. www.newscientist.com/article/2140576-video-stored-in-live-bacterial-genome-using-crispr-gene-editing.
12. www.livescience.com/62569-mammoth-elephant-hybrid-help-climate.html.
13. www.sciencedirect.com/science/article/pii/S1044579X17302742.
14. Jennifer Doudna Samuel Sternberg, A Crack in Creation: Gene Editing and the Unthinkable Power to Control Evolution, 2018.

CHAPTER 2

WHAT IS THE PURPOSE?

The human brain processes many millions of bits per second, but only a fraction of the signals reach our consciousness.[1] Some of the key filters that sort out signals to the brain are human biases.[2] From an evolutionary point of view, biases are smart because they act as thumb rules (also called heuristics) and make it faster and easier for us to navigate life (Daniel Kahneman and Amos Tversky were the first to chart a large number of human biases. To dive deeper into this fascinating subject, I recommend a close reading of their work).[3] But the problem is that the rules of thumb, that we believe are helpful to us, are very often wrong.

Here are just a few examples of how our brain biases cheat us: we all have an optimism bias, which means that we, as humans, are overoptimistic about our own future and basically think things are going to be better for us in the future than they have been in the past. This is also where the 'well, that would never happen to me' mindset lies. Paradoxically, there are actually analyses that show that one of the causes of successful people's good fortune is that they have such an immense optimism bias that they are able to convince others about their future success and that this optimism thereby becomes a self-fulfilling prophecy. For example, a survey among professional swimmers found that the swimmers who had a tendency towards self-deception also performed better.[4] Some believe that overdeveloped optimism biases are not insignificant reasons behind Steve Jobs and Elon Musk's huge successes. Nevertheless, the optimism bias also causes us to tend to not take good care of ourselves, to fail to save up for retirement, to not stop smoking, to not exercise, and to not develop an ambitious strategy for our businesses.

We humans also have a proximity bias that causes us to interpret events that have happened recently as more likely than events that happened a long time ago. After a terrorist attack, people believe that a new terrorist attack will occur sooner than is statistically justifiable. When there has been a recent earthquake, people believe that a new earthquake will strike. And once you have been successful in the stock market, you think it is more likely that you will soon succeed in the stock market once again.

We also have a confirmation bias. This means that we mostly listen to information that confirms our pre-existing convictions (a bias that social media helps to reinforce). Then we have a hindsight bias that causes us to exaggerate our 'I-knew-this-would-happen' response after an event has taken place. Our outcome bias makes us praise the manager when things are going well and scold them when things are bad; this is not based on how sensible the manager's decision was before we knew the outcome, but on the results. The halo effect causes us to ascribe good motives to the politician we like, and believe in their position more strongly than in that of the politician we don't like. Regardless of the facts. And, in fact, there is also research that shows that we are more likely to vote for the politician who has the biggest mouth.[5] The status quo bias means that we humans prefer to 'not lose' over winning. That is to say, we prefer to maintain our current situation. Likewise, the omission bias means that we tend to prefer inactivity over activity.[6] In other words, we would rather not act than act. Therefore, people need to be persuaded with strong arguments to participate in projects where the result is unknown. And that is always the case when we talk about innovation. 'Sunk-cost fallacy' is a type of bias that makes it very hard to give something up once we've invested a large amount of time or money in it, even when it would be the right thing to do. Among other things, this is why established companies have so many legacy systems that they are always late to upgrade. The list is long. And interestingly, Kahneman and Tversky's experiments show that statisticians and scientists, who otherwise make their living conducting in-depth analyses, make the same mistakes and fall victim to exactly the same biases as we common mortals do.

Evolution has given us all our biases because they make the world simpler and enable us to act intuitively, which is smart if you are in situations where you need to react quickly to survive. But in today's society, the biases have gone and become less vital, because in the West, at least, we no longer live at constant risk of mortal danger. We must, therefore, be aware of our biases so that we can manage them better. Because if we are not aware of the biases of our minds, which often make us draw the wrong conclusions and perform insufficient analyses, then we will make the wrong choices.

Just as biases act as rules of thumb and simplify the world for us, so do stories. Stories or narratives help us make decisions. They help us navigate, and they motivate us because stories are images of reality that make things more comprehensible and present to us. Therefore, the brain also pays more attention to the greater narrative and how well it is told, than it does to concrete facts and to the likelihood that the stories we are told are true.

It is therefore important that you have a story in your company, a narrative that employees and customers can understand and identify with, to motivate them and counter the biases that would otherwise hold them back. In the book *Exponential Organizations*,[7] Salim Ismail and his co-authors speak about having a massive transformative purpose, which is exactly that kind of story. If you have a massive transformative purpose (also called an MTP), you have a fundamental purpose beyond simply making your shareholders richer, increasing top and bottom lines, or selling more items. All the exponential organizations that the authors identified in their analyses – businesses like Airbnb, Google, and Apple that are defined as organizations with a particular ability to create results that are not only ten percent better, but ten times better than traditional companies – proved to have a massive transformative purpose. Having an MTP is the same as having a big story in your organization.

My favourite example of an MTP is Tesla's. Its massive transformative purpose is 'accelerating the world's transition to sustainable energy'. The goal is not about electric cars – it's much bigger than that. All Tesla employees know the purpose. And not only do they know it – they are also navigating based on it. Because people are highly motivated by the chance to help make a difference. And the massive transformative purpose is a narrative that awakens a strong inner sense of motivation – unlike external motivators such as money and status – and a desire to help, to do something for others, to help make a difference, and to be a better person. It may sound like some kind of flower power sentimentality, but massive transformative purposes are far stronger motivators for people than monetary rewards. This is also increasingly reflected in the younger generations – among those we call millennials. A recent American study showed that 70% of millennials were willing to be paid lower salaries to work for a company that makes a difference in the world.[8]

Many established organizations have no massive transformative purpose. Their so-called visions are semi-statistical formulations about being among the three leading companies in their industry within a geographically defined area or something similar. Such a vision is not very ambitious nor motivational, because it does not speak to us as human beings. It does not contain a strong narrative. Over the years, in working with many different established organizations, I have met companies that have something that is reminiscent of a massive transformative purpose. That's the purpose that has been a part of their

WHAT IS THE PURPOSE?

DNA since they were founded 50, 100, or many more years ago. Sometimes these purposes even feature nicely on websites and in brochures, but they remain invisible in the company's daily operations and thus do not come into their own as motivational factors for the employees. It's almost as if it's been forgotten that the massive transformative purpose is different from, and more than, an advertising message for the marketing department. But if you incorporate your purpose into your daily life, it can be a very powerful tool. All Tesla employees know what they go to work to create. They do it to accelerate the world's transition to sustainable energy. They are reminded of the purpose almost daily, and it is a decisive driving force for both daily operations and innovation.

Several other analyses support how important it is for an organization to have a higher purpose that everyone in the organization knows about, and that such a purpose has a spillover effect, both on the belief in the company's future and on financial outcomes. A Deloitte study with more than 1000 respondents showed, among other things, that companies whose employees have a strong sense of purpose also believe more strongly that the company will develop in a positive direction (82% vs. 42% in companies without this experience of a major purpose) and believe that they will remain competitive in the future (83% vs. 42%).[9] The extent to which employees' faith in the future of their businesses also translates into results is, of course, a different story. Here, the other parameters, which the higher purpose is paired with, play a decisive role. This was shown in a big meta-analysis that was performed by George Serafeim, Andrea Prat, and Claudine Gartenberg. They took the results from 429 US companies' responses to the 'Great Places to Work' survey, which is a global analysis where companies can volunteer to have employee satisfaction levels measured, and analysed more than 450,000 responses to find out if there is a direct correlation between companies where employees experience a higher purpose and their financial performance. Here, the analyses showed that there is a correlation between the experience of a higher purpose and the economic results of those organizations where there were also clear objectives from management (identified by level of agreement with statements in the survey, such as 'Management has a clear picture of where organization must go'). The analysts call these 'purpose-clarity organizations'. Conversely, they did not see any connection between higher-purpose organizations and a 'culture of camaraderie' (revealed through agreement with statements such as 'There is a family or team spirit in the organization'), which did not simultaneously show clear management goals. These companies are called 'purpose-camaraderie organizations'. Thus, the analysis indicates that goal achievement coupled with a higher purpose is more important for a company's financial performance than the experience of a friendly work culture coupled with a higher purpose.

Does that mean that a positive working culture is insignificant? No, of course not, and, later, we will also look at the importance of creating a positive working culture to creating well-functioning teams and a strong innovation culture. However, in relation to companies' overall economic performance, a higher purpose paired with clear objectives is the determining combination. What's equally interesting is the fact that the analysis indicates that specialists and middle managers' attitudes to these parameters are crucial to the correlation between purpose, clarity of objectives, and economic results. But neither part-time employees (which, I guess, intuitively makes sense) nor top management[10] affect the outcome. The latter may seem surprising and thought-provoking, if you are a top executive.

Narratives, storytelling in the form of a greater purpose for the organization, and a massive transformative purpose motivate us as human beings and help us overcome some of our biases, one of the most important being our status quo bias, which slows us in our development and innovation. Therefore, organizations should find their great story and incorporate it into their culture and workflows.

NOTES

1. Tor Nørretranders, The User Illusion, 1999.
2. Steven Kotler and Jamie Wheal, Stealing Fire, 2017; and Steven Kotler, The Rise of Superman, 2014.

3. Daniel Kahneman, Thinking Fast and Slow, 2010.
4. Kevin Simler and Robin Hanson, The Elephant in the Brain, 2018; and Starek and Keating, Self-deception and its relationship to success in competition, 1991.
5. Experiment conducted by Dr Roeland Dietvorst.
6. Calestous Juma, Innovation and Its Enemies, 2016.
7. Salim Ismail, Exponential Organizations, 2014.
8. www.conecomm.com/news-blog/2016-cone-communications-millennial-employee-engagement-study-press-release.
9. www2.deloitte.com/content/dam/Deloitte/us/Documents/about-deloitte/us-leadership-2014-core-beliefs-culture-survey-040414.pdf.
10. Claudine Madras Gartenberg, Andrea Prat, and George Serafeim, Corporate Purpose and Financial Performance (June 30, 2016). Organization Science. https://ssrn.com/abstract=2840005 or http://dx.doi.org/10.2139/ssrn.2840005.

CHAPTER 3

WHICH INDUSTRY AM I IN?

Once upon a time, the question 'Which industry am I really in?' was easy to answer. You were in the business of law and sold legal assistance, or in the banking world and provided financing, or in the shipping industry and moved goods from point A to point B. But in a world where not only technologies, but whole industries, converge, the answer is no longer so obvious. This industry convergence means that competitors can come from many different places today, but it also means that the potential for developing one's organization has changed significantly. Let's look at a company like Amazon that understands this better than most, and has the trait of constant development deeply rooted in its DNA.

As is well known, Amazon was initially a bookseller that sold physical books online. However, in 2007, they launched Kindle, the e-reader for digital books. Kindle was designed to disrupt the physical book. But it did not happen. The reason was, in my opinion, that the product simply was not good enough. This applies not only to Kindle, but to all e-readers. E-readers did not, and still do not, create such a good customer experience that they can replace the feeling many get from reading a physical book. What often happens when new media are introduced is that they more or less directly copy the old media. The first movie in the world was simply theatre caught on film. You set up a camera, filmed the play and then showed it to an audience on a canvas. The first websites of the early 1990s were designed in exactly the same way as the companies' physical brochures. And e-pub book files, which can be read on Kindle, etc., are largely like physical books that have been scanned and stored in a digital device. There are, of course, conveniences to enjoy with e-readers. For instance, you can save many books at once without being weighed down, but the new medium is still immature and we have not yet seen it use the potential to create better experiences than physical books can. People who read e-books also do not achieve the same level of results as those who read books on paper. My company completed an analysis in 2016 with one of the world's leading neuroanalysis companies, Neurons Inc., where we put electrodes on 30 study participants' heads to measure brain activity when they read a physical book, and a book on a tablet, cell phone, and laptop. Respondents were most able to remember what they had read in the physical book, and this was also when they were most emotionally engaged. So overall, e-readers did not have the impact that many thought they would. E-readers did not disrupt the physical book. If anything were to make the physical book a niche medium, it would be something that combines reading with augmented and virtual reality, allowing for the addition of new levels of visual, auditory, and interactive layers to the reading. But there is still some way to go to reach that point.

However, regardless of the e-readers' shortcomings, Kindle was a great success for Amazon and, along with the increasing need for Amazon to scale up and build third-party websites to support their e-commerce,[1] Amazon's need to find new data storage solutions grew massively. Therefore, they invented Amazon Web Services or AWS (data storage in the cloud).[2] AWS was initially an internal product that was meant to service Amazon itself, but as the product matured, it started being introduced to customers. Today, AWS turns a profit of over $17 billion[3] and is the primary reason why Amazon is in the black, something that Amazon has otherwise notoriously been uninterested in, since the company has always chased growth over profitability. Although AWS is a part of Amazon, it is also established as its own independent business, as activity in this part of Amazon is radically different from what is done in the more traditional retail segment. We return to this principle in Chapter 12 on mutating innovation, which is crucial for achieving success with new strategic efforts when using competencies, technologies, and business models that are substantially different from those traditionally used.

With extensive digitization, Amazon's need to establish data centres also increased, and data centres need large amounts of energy. So Amazon created Amazon Wind Power, which builds and operates its own wind farms and services their own data centres (just like they have also set up solar farms). In collaboration with the wind turbine manufacturer GE, Amazon recently established a 400-million-dollar wind farm in Texas with a capacity of one million annual megawatt hours, which also enables them to supply energy to 90,000 private households.[4] So now, Amazon is also an energy company.

Moreover, Amazon has expanded its hardware activities with various profitable products over the past five years, which, other than a significantly unsuccessful smartphone, also includes the hugely successful Echo, the device that provides a customer-facing artificial intelligence service through Alexa. According to the company, they sold millions of Echos[5] during the Christmas period alone in 2017. Amazon has also established Amazon Studios, which produces movies and shows, and has even won its first Oscars. North America's second-largest fashion outlet is owned by Amazon; it also serves as a third-party distribution centre for the world's big and small product manufacturers. Amazon has even invested in its first biotech company, Grail, which is working to develop new methods for diagnosing cancer.[6]

In other words, Amazon continuously reinvents – or mutates – the organization to make it stronger and more competitive by constantly exploring what further actions they can take to translate their skills into value to customers. These strategic initiative domains are established through own developments as well as acquisitions but share a starting point in the value that the organization currently creates, while at the same time challenging the core business and moving away from it. It may sound paradoxical, but the principle can be seen in the creation of Kindle: the organization, being an established bookseller, knew it was logical to explore how to digitize the book, because Amazon knew that if they did not, someone else would. Or as with AWS, there was, due to digitization, a great need for better and cheaper solutions for the organization to store data, and customers had this need as well. As an extremely customer-centric organization, it was therefore natural for Amazon to further develop the solution for customers.

Google, which was established in 1998,[7] is another example of a business that is only 20 years old but has actually already mutated several times. Google's starting point was Internet searches. These are what made Google big. But the thing that made Google really big, and which is its definitive core business today, is advertising. The shift from search to advertising was Google's first mutation, i.e. a radical change in core business. In parallel, Google began experimenting with other initiatives, such as developing self-driving cars, investing in startups, and conducting health research. These activities led Google to breaking up the company in its second mutation and, thereby, establishing its third basic structure within the space of just 20 years, when Google changed its name to Alphabet in 2015[8] to create a stronger organizational structure that gave more room for the new ventures while simultaneously not disturbing the core business of the old Google and its advertising and search.

Apple has also mutated several times. From personal computers, which were the starting point for the core business, to iPods and iPhones, which currently account for well over 80% of the organization's revenue.[9] The question is what Apple's next mutation will be. We do not know. Perhaps they are moving into the health sector, carried by their iWatches, which collect data about the health of users. Perhaps they will develop software for self-driving cars, which has been a major priority for some years; however, only a few insiders really know what the future holds for this. Wherever Apple moves, they know that if they are to remain one of the world's most valuable companies, the core will have to mutate.

This book's research indicates that all companies – if they want to maintain, or exceed, their levels of success 10, 20, 30 years from now – have to explore how they can mutate so that the core of the organization will look different. This involves a great tolerance for uncertainty and many experiments, which we will return to. But, before we reach that point, let us continue to look at how we can sharpen the axe and explore some of the key issues that are crucial to implementing the right strategy.

NOTES

1. John Rossman, The Amazon Way on IoT, 2016; and Brad Stone, The Everything Store, 2014.
2. https://aws.amazon.com/?nc2=h_lg.
3. http://nordic.businessinsider.com/amazon-web-services-2017-revenue-2018-2?r=US&IR=T.
4. www.ge.com/reports/amazon-turns-ge-wind-turbines-power-business.
5. www.cnbc.com/2017/12/26/how-many-amazon-alexa-echoes-were-sold-over-the-2017-holidays.html.
6. CB Insights Amazon strategic breakdown, 2018.
7. https://en.wikipedia.org/wiki/Google.
8. https://en.wikipedia.org/wiki/Alphabet_Inc.
9. https://9to5mac.com/2018/05/01/apple-earnings-fy18-q2.

CHAPTER 4

WHAT DO CUSTOMERS WANT?

In 2016, I published the book *The Fundamental 4s: How to Design Extraordinary Customer Experiences in an Exponential World* with my partner Laila Pawlak. The book was the result of many years of customer analyses and research into human motivation, and how to create stronger customer experiences through a deeper understanding of people's basic driving forces. What do customers really want? Most organizations spend a lot of energy trying to understand this. More and more organizations incorporate customer centricity in their value set and make 'customer first' the focal point of their strategies. But often, there isn't enough of a basic understanding of what is most important to the customer. An understanding that is a fundamental tool for creating valuable customer-oriented initiatives, and an understanding that can simultaneously be turned inward and used internally within the organization to motivate employees. Because customers and employees share the fact that they are people, and the things that fundamentally motivate us as customers are the same things that motivate us as human beings. So let's look at the motivations that drive us as human beings, which we have called The Fundamental 4s, because they are fundamental and there are four of them.[1]

As shown in Model 1, we have named the four core motivations BE, DO, FEEL, and LOOK with the common denominator 'better', because all of our core motivations share the fact that they are part of mankind's fundamental drive towards self-improvement. All people, whether they are aware of it or not, are on a constant life journey towards becoming better people. Whether it's the baby's stubborn experimentation with crawling, standing, and walking, or the child playing, the young person's exam revision, the adult's career moves, or the senior's golf practice, all these activities have in common that they are part of the human journey of development. Having said that, inherent in this journey are various basic motives that may be stronger or weaker, depending on what we are doing. The four basic motives differ from each other by being comparatively proactive or reactive, as well as intrinsic or extrinsic. Let me give a quick theoretical overview below and then exemplify:

- The BE better motivation is about our values and moral landscapes – the things that matter to us as human beings. This motivation is intrinsic and proactive. That is to say, we fulfil the motivation within ourselves by virtue of the things we do, such as donating to charity, buying organic eggs for animal welfare purposes, or helping other people.
- The DO better motivation is about our results, competencies, and skills. It is proactive and extrinsic. You make something happen and it manifests itself extrinsically by, e.g. generating results at work, developing your physique through exercise, or making you smarter through studying.
- The FEEL better motivation is all about what you can see, feel, hear, smell, taste, sense. It is intrinsic and reactive. One is influenced by external stimuli, such as heat, light, sound, a room's design or a product's design, and it stimulates a feeling.
- The LOOK better motivation is about social status. It is reactive and extrinsic. Something happens to you and the reward lies outside of yourself; it could, for instance, be a diploma or 'likes' on Facebook.

All four motivations are important to us as humans, but in certain situations, some motivations will be stronger than others.

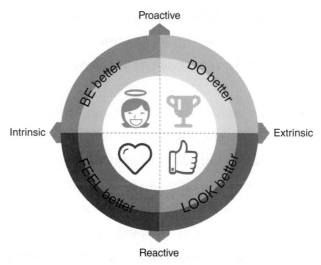

Model 1 Human Beings' Four Basic Motivations
Source: Laila Pawlak & Kris Østergaard

If you as an organization develop products and services, you want to make sure that you understand which of these motivations are most important to the product or service you have developed, how to ideally honour all four motivations, and how to ensure that you do not demotivate the recipient by having them BE, DO, FEEL, or LOOK worse. Let's look at some examples to make the theory more tangible.

The BE better motivation, which concerns our values and moral landscapes, is becoming increasingly important. Earlier in the book, when we discussed the strength of having a massive transformative purpose and using Tesla's MTP as an example – accelerating the world's transition to sustainable energy – part of the explanation for the strength of this MTP is that it causes Tesla's employees to BE better. They feel like better people by contributing to making a positive difference in the world – a feeling they would not even come close to achieving just by helping to make their business one of the top three suppliers of electric cars. An increasing number of companies are born with a strong BE better profile.

One of the best examples of this, which we also emphasized in our original book on the subject, is Be My Eyes,[2] a platform for the blind and visually impaired. With the help of an app, blind or visually impaired people can get help with sight via a video connection to helpers who are also connected to the platform. The blind or visually impaired person uses the video function of the app to contact one of the more than 2 million helpers worldwide and, through the video connection, they can ask for help with distinguishing apple juice from tomato juice in the supermarket, navigating a store, or reading a letter out loud. In fact, Be My Eyes has become the world's largest community for the blind and visually impaired, a status they achieved after only having been online for six months. The reason that Be My Eyes has achieved this is that the helpers on the platform get a strong sense of being good people when they give help. We all know that feeling. Different analyses even show that people find giving to others more valuable than giving to ourselves.[3] Looking at some of the testimonials that the Be My Eyes helpers put on their social media shows how strong the motivation of helping someone is, and how much value it creates. One helper wrote on Pinterest: 'I just got my first Be My Eyes request. A man from Iraq needed help reading his health and birth documents. I feel so fulfilled I could cry.' Imagine if your company's customers said the same about you.

If you were cynical – which you should not be, but let's just momentarily explore this for the sake of argument – then the person who described their experience on social media just worked for free for Be My Eyes. But the person did not feel that he/she worked for free, because the value in helping someone else, in BEing better, was far stronger than any monetary reward could be. The BE better motivation is also a major part of the driving force behind the increasing volume of voluntary work that people perform in their free time and in connection with their jobs. The same is true in platform economies like Airbnb where you open your home to others, or you support an exciting project on the crowdfunding platform Kickstarter (other motivations are also met, but the BE better part is highly represented), or when a rising number of companies build their strategies around the UN's sustainable development goals.

The DO better motivation, which concerns our results, competencies, and skills, is the motivation that most organizations spend the most energy fulfilling. It's about making things faster, smarter, bigger, or more convenient. A GPS is a DO better product. It puts us in a better position to get from point A to point B. The whole digital revolution is a DO better revolution. Most of your smartphone apps are DO better apps; they increase your results, competencies, or skills, whether it's the meditation app, the flashlight, the payment app, Messenger, or something else. It is probably obvious to all why it is important to honour this motivation with one's customers (or employees for that matter). If we do not help our customers DO, then our services are likely to have limited value.

The importance of the FEEL better and LOOK better motivations is not always obvious to organizations. FEEL better is about our sensory experiences. LOOK better is about our social status. The probability that you own an Apple product is quite high if you live in the Western part of the world with a minimum middle-sized income. If you have an Apple product, you may also remember when you purchased your Apple product. How did it feel? The packaging? Opening the box? Seeing and holding the well-designed product the first time? You can probably feel it right now, just thinking about it. I once organized a focus group with a bunch of Apple lovers. It was at the time when the first iPhone had just been launched in Denmark. One of the participants told me how, when she went to bed at night, she would ritually pet her Mac and say goodnight to it, as if it were a completely natural thing to do. Because it made her FEEL better. She also had no boyfriend at the time, so maybe there was a connection there. But one cannot underestimate the importance of creating sensory appeal for people. That's what we do when we put candles on the table. It's not because we can't see, but because it's cosy. That's what music does to us. This is a significant explanation for why the decor in our home and at our jobs is crucial to our well-being. And that is why we talk about 'eating with your eyes'.

One of the strongest examples I've experienced of how valuable honouring the FEEL better motivation can be as a design principle comes from the healthcare sector. MR scanners that scan both brain and body are very big and noisy machines in which you have to lie completely still to be scanned. In other words, it can be a rather claustrophobic and scary experience to be scanned – especially when you are a child. In fact, analyses have shown that up to 80% of all smaller children undergoing an MR study need tranquilizers before they dare enter the big noisy machines. Doug Dietz, an industrial designer working for GE Healthcare (a producer of MR scanners) made that observation as well. It made him consider what he could do to make the experience less scary for children, thus limiting the need to give them tranquilizers before they got scanned. The solution turned out to be very simple. It wasn't about the development of new technology that would remove the noise, or technology that would completely eliminate the need to lie inside a scanner. It was about seeing the experience through the eyes of the children. Normally, MR scanners are placed in clinical white hospital premises, and they usually are white. Dietz thought it would be too expensive and difficult to change the machine, but what if they could change the environment instead? So Dietz and his team painted a whole room and the scanner into a pirate adventure, where the children would walk the plank to the scanner. Shipwrecks were painted on the walls, water was painted on the floor and a treasure chest was painted in the corner.[4] The result was surprising. Instead of 80% of the children having tranquilizers before scanning, the numbers were reversed, with only 27% needing tranquilizers.[5] Because the children had been made to FEEL better. An experience that appealed to the senses was created, and it outweighed the anxiety-inducing part of the process – by using paint. Today, GE Healthcare has transformed this discovery into a series of products that they call their Adventure Series and they have created a wide variety of scenarios in which their products feature.[6]

The LOOK better motivation, our need for social status, is a motivation that we tend to ignore or even proactively argue against in Denmark and in the Nordic region where I am from. That's because of 'the Law of Jante', which is a very strong cultural norm in my region of the world that states that 'you should not think you are anything'. But no matter how strong the Law of

Jante is, the LOOK better motivation is even stronger. Because we all need social recognition. People are social animals, and therefore we need the recognition of other people. Perhaps the most obvious proof of this is our behaviour on social media and the need to get likes on Facebook and other social media. A 'like' on Facebook is equal to social recognition. It is a very tangible piece of evidence that other people acknowledge an act or attitude positively by assigning value to a social media post in the form of a 'like'. That's also why likes are addictive; every time you get a like, the neurotransmitter dopamine is released in the brain. Dopamine is also known as the 'sex, drugs and rock 'n' roll molecule'[7] because it makes us happy and is released when you win games, take drugs, drink alcohol – and use social media. There are even studies that show that exclusion from social activity causes a form of 'social pain' that activates the same areas in the brain that are associated with physical pain.[8] That's why it hurts if you post something on Facebook and it does not get any likes. It is experienced as being left out. An organization such as Facebook is extremely aware of these mechanisms, which raises a number of ethical issues in relation to how addictive one should make one's products. Should you, as a manufacturer of a product, try to indiscriminately increase your users' consumption, or should you try to create balanced consumption? That is a tough standard to hold producers to, because virtually all companies have the sub-goal of increasing consumption of their products and services, whether it's Facebook, app developers, game producers, televisions, or banks. But, nevertheless, it is an important question to consider.

My favourite example of a company that has deliberately worked with the LOOK better motivation as a force for good is the software company Opower, which was acquired by Oracle in 2016. Opower developed customer service software for the energy industry and developed solutions to motivate consumers to save energy, as many energy companies around the world are required to do by law. That's why you see some, in my view, failed TV commercials from energy companies about how to save energy, trying to motivate customers to save about a few hundred dollars a year by turning on and off all their electrical appliances throughout the house every day. But it's simply too much effort for too little reward for it to affect people's behaviour. What Opower did, however, was to develop algorithms to measure the individual consumer's domestic energy consumption, thus providing targeted recommendations for how the customer could save energy. The ingenious thing about this was that Opower simultaneously informed their customers about how much energy they consumed compared to their neighbours. Because if there is one thing you would want to do in life, it's to beat the neighbour. By providing this information, customers were given the opportunity to 'LOOK better' compared to their neighbours. Overall, Opower managed to influence the final consumption of end consumers by 2.5% using these methods.[9]

As mentioned, the four basic motivations we have reviewed are not equally important for all products and services. The restaurant industry will probably always focus more on the FEEL better motivation than production companies will. The fashion industry will probably always focus more on the LOOK better motivation than most other industries. And so on, and so forth. But the more you can honour all four motivations and, at the very least, make sure that you do not make people BE, DO, FEEL, or LOOK worse, the stronger the experience and the more value you can create. This insight should be incorporated into your products and services to create stronger customer experiences. You should also use it to create stronger employee experiences. You can also get your employees to BE, DO, FEEL, and LOOK better, creating a strong corporate culture with highly motivated people. You can even consider using the principles at home and get your partner, spouse and/or children to BE, DO, FEEL, and LOOK better, thus creating an even more harmonious home (just a thought: maybe don't tell them that that's what you're doing).

In summary, the better we understand human motivation, the more value we can create, and in a world of constant change with ever-increasing competition, we need to continuously increase value.

NOTES

1. You can study the subject further by visiting www.fundamental4s.com and downloading a free version of the full book.
2. www.bemyeyes.com.
3. www.theguardian.com/science/2008/mar/21/medicalresearch.usa.
4. https://thisisdesignthinking.net/2014/12/changing-experiences-through-empathy-ge-healthcares-adventure-series.
5. http://archive.jsonline.com/business/by-turning-medical-scans-into-adventures-ge-eases-childrens-fears-b99647870z1-366161191.html.
6. www.gehealthcare.com/en/products/accessories-and-supplies/adventure-series-for-x-ray.
7. www.theguardian.com/technology/2018/mar/04/has-dopamine-got-us-hooked-on-tech-facebook-apps-addiction.
8. https://hbr.org/2012/05/your-brain-on-facebook; http://www.pnas.org/content/early/2011/03/22/1102693108.
9. www.bloomberg.com/news/articles/2009-11-09/energy-use-neighbor-vs-dot-neighbor.

CHAPTER 5

WHO ARE MY COMPETITORS?

No fintech startup in its right mind has the strategy of disrupting a bank. No gifted insurtech startup starts out wanting to make insurance companies redundant. No intelligent healthcare startup plans to put all pharmaceutical companies out of business. It's too complicated and doomed to fail. The question to ask yourself as a startup is not how to disrupt a business. The question is how to eat an elephant, and the answer is, as you know: one bite at a time. Smart startups focus on one problem, one value-creating service, one process worth optimizing, one potentially transformative experience, and then do everything they can to become world champions in just that. That is why innovation is much easier for them than it is for established companies. A startup has one job.

Over the years, I have carried out many qualitative and quantitative analyses with entrepreneurs to understand what drives them. And if there's one thing I've heard over and over again in those analyses, it's a sentence that, in the simplest and most beautiful way, demonstrates the basic motivation most entrepreneurs have for embarking on their start-up adventure: 'There's got to be a better way. . .'. A problem, a nuisance, an unfulfilling experience, a product that did not do what its marketing promised, coupled with someone who did not just sweep the problem under the carpet or settled with writing a complaint to customer service or a negative review on Yelp, but was so annoyed by the perceived imperfection that they decided to do better. That's basically what entrepreneurship is about. A startup does not look at Maersk, Google, Procter & Gamble, or Telia, and develop a strategy to surpass them. They look at each and every one of the products or services that these established players offer, and then they explore how they can do just one thing better. And you can rest assured that, for each service and for each product that exists in your company's product portfolio, there are – literally – hundreds of startups worldwide, maybe even thousands, working to provide exactly that service or product at least ten times better.

Do you know all the thousands of startups that challenge your company's products and services on the international stage? Of course not. How could you. But it's crucial that you get to that stage. Or, rather, that at least some people in your business do. Not that you have to get to know everyone, but you must know the most important ones, and you can do that if you establish partnerships with the ecosystems that actually know the many thousands of entrepreneurs. Enterprise ecosystems include accelerators such as Plug and Play, Singularity University's Global Startup Program, TechStars, 500 Startups, and Y Combinator, which annually receive thousands of applications from startups across the world to participate in their accelerator programmes, where entrepreneurs have a few months to work intensively to find customers and investments, develop business models and basically make their businesses more viable. Only a fraction of the entrepreneurs that apply to join the accelerator programmes are accepted and therefore, to some extent, they can be expected to be the most relevant startups at that moment in time.

You can also work with the co-working spaces that are mushrooming in all major cities, and now also in smaller ones. In Copenhagen alone, a city with less than a million inhabitants, there are more than 65 co-working spaces.[1] Each of the co-working spaces has a better sense of what is happening on the startup scene than the established companies do with their headquarters in city centres or suburbs, because they get to know the many entrepreneurs really well. Therefore, a bridge must be built between startup-land and corporate headquarters, wherever they are, via the ecosystems. These partnerships are important to the established player. Not only to identify potential future competitors, but also to identify potential future partners, so they won't have to reinvent the wheel themselves. We will look at that dimension later.

But even when the big organizations scan the startup world for potential competitors, they are still only scratching the surface of the competitive landscape. To get a full overview and reap new knowledge, you have to explore your competitive landscape in a slightly different way. This can be done by playing a game I call 'six degrees of competition'.

Throughout the twentieth century, both authors and scientists all around the world explored social networks and the influence of technological development on human connections. The Hungarian author Frigyes Karinthy studied the phenomenon in the story *Chains*[2] from 1929 where he played with the idea that, thanks to technological development, the world had become smaller and that all people could be linked by very few connectors. Psychologist Stanley Milgram[3] was inspired by the story to investigate the phenomenon known as the 'small world' problem in 1967, when he sent letters to 160 different people in the United States and asked them to forward the letters to the acquaintances they thought would bring the letters closest to one ultimate recipient, a stockbroker in Boston. The first letter wound up with the stockbroker within four days with only two stops along the way and, at the end of the experiment, Milgram found that each letter made five stops on average. Hence, the phrase 'six degrees of separation' that you may be familiar with.[4] The point here is that the world is getting smaller and smaller, and that the connections between us are becoming shorter and shorter.

If you take the 'small world' principle and apply it to your competitors, something interesting happens. In the exercise I would like to introduce to you now the idea is to take one core product or service as a starting point. Let us suppose we are coffee producers and use 400 grams of packaged ground coffee beans as an example. With inspiration from Milgram's experiment, we can now trace the 400 grams of ground coffee beans and explore who or what the closest competitor is in the first degree, and then who or what the closest competitor is in second degree, and continue up to sixth degree and then see if we can close the chain and lead the sixth degree competitor back to the starting point – the 400 grams of packaged ground coffee beans.

Let's say that the 400 grams of ground coffee beans are from Folgers. It could be any coffee brand. But let's just choose Folgers, as it is one of the best-selling coffee brands in the world.

If you were to point out the first degree of competition to 400 grams of Folgers coffee beans, who or what would it be?

If your suggestion is other coffee brands like Nescafe, Maxwell House, Keurig, or Gevalia, who also sell packaged ground coffee beans, we are on the same wavelength. It is basically the same product, in the same packaging, for the same price with the same value. So far, so good. Who would be competitors in the second degree to ground coffee beans?

My suggestion would be tea or maybe other hot drinks, but probably tea. If you drink a cup of hot tea, you are busy not drinking a cup of hot coffee, and you are thereby not using any of your ground coffee beans. Who would be the third degree competitor?

What about Red Bull? Or Coca-Cola or other soda-like drinks. But especially Red Bull and Cola. They are cold, not hot, but they contain incredible amounts of caffeine, and in many ways they are oriented towards the same kind of value creation as the coffee is: giving the recipient more energy. Who would be the fourth degree competitor?

Here, I usually start getting fewer and more diverse responses from the audience when I give presentations around the world and play this game with them. The answer will be everything from caffeine pills to red wine (which, however, does not have the same effect on me as coffee, but maybe it's just me) to drugs and sleep. And sometimes the suggestion is the same as mine, namely Starbucks. If you buy a cup of coffee at Starbucks, then you are not using the ground beans that you would prepare to make a cup of steamy hot coffee; rather, you are choosing to let Starbucks do it. Who could the fifth degree competitor be?

Here, it becomes difficult for people to guess, because we are well on our way out of the comfort zone and into unknown territory. But allow me to make a few suggestions. Have you heard of a Thync?[5] Thync calls itself a 'wearable', which creates peace and energy and is an electronic device that you place on your head. The original version of Thync has two settings. One setting sends electronic signals to the brain to make the brain's owner more relaxed. The other sends electronic signals to the brain to give the brain's owner more energy. I've tried it myself, and it kind of works. You can use a Thync for 10–15 minutes and let it stimulate the brain to experience an energy boost.

Or what about a Muse,[6] a meditation unit that is attached to the forehead and behind the ears? It does not send electronic signals to the brain, but it reads brain waves and decodes whether the brain is in an alpha, beta, or theta state. In other words, it tells you how relaxed you are. Via an app, you can choose different soundscapes like rainforest, beach, or city streets, and, using headphones, you can listen your way to your brain's activity level. The more relaxed you are, the less noise there is and the less the wind blows in the various soundscapes. If you hear birds chirping, you know that you are completely zen and have achieved the optimal condition. The information is tracked, of course, to measure your development. It's gamified meditation in a convenient way. I can't help but think about what products like Thync and Muse or other similar products on the market are going to do to coffee cup no. 3, 4, 5, and 6 over the course of a day if you, instead of grabbing a cup of coffee and a Snickers bar at 3 p.m. for a few extra hours of focus, put on your wearable for ten minutes and reap the same rewards. And the products available today are only version 1.0. Imagine where we might be headed.

Who could be the sixth degree of competition to 400 grams of ground coffee beans from Folgers? When we reach this point in the chain of questions, there's usually complete silence. But think about electric cars and ultimately self-driving cars. In just a few years, only electric cars will be produced. All major automakers are in the process of converting their production, and the global fleet will be replaced by electric cars over time. In our part of the world, it will probably go fast. Within a few years, self-driving cars will also be a normal feature in traffic. How will our coffee needs be affected when we have self-driving cars and no longer need to drink coffee to be vigilant enough to focus on traffic? It might mean a lot, or it might not.

Perhaps we will still want to drink the same amount of coffee, but we will have a better time enjoying it because we wouldn't simultaneously need to focus on holding a steering wheel and keeping an eye on other (stupid) drivers. But one thing is for sure: Electric cars and self-driving cars will massively impact the coffee producers' value chain. Because where is a large proportion of the revenue of coffee producers, Starbucks, and Red Bull coming from? From gas stations. With electric cars and particularly self-driving cars, we will no longer have to think about gas. Bang! With a blow, the world has radically changed. Because if we no longer need to go to the gas station, where are coffee producers, Starbucks, Red Bull, and the many other on-the-go-dependent brands going to sell their products? And that is how the self-driving car goes on to become the coffee producer's future sixth degree of competition.

Are the board members of the coffee producers discussing Thync, Muse, electric and self-driving cars? I don't know. I have exclusively used them to illustrate an example. But I would venture to assert that very few boards, management groups, product development teams, and analytics units in most established organizations have those discussions. They never go further than the second, third, or maximum fourth degree before feeling confident they have an overview of their competitors. However, I know that Red Bull does. They continually explore the fifth, sixth, and maybe even the seventh degree of competition to make sure they understand threats and opportunities so they can prepare themselves properly for the future.

I challenge you to take your own core product and go through the same exercise. Ask yourself: 'How do you digitize a cup of coffee?' Or rather, find out what your version is of this strange question, depending on whatever type of core service you are examining. Who are your competitors in the fourth, fifth, and sixth degree? That place where you leave your comfort zone and the answers are no longer obvious. This investigation will significantly expand your competitive landscape and, more importantly, it will illustrate an opportunity space that is many times greater than what your organization is traditionally oriented to. An opportunity space where it even becomes logical for coffee producers to potentially go ahead and develop digital services, and to completely reconsider their distribution chains.

You must dare to ask such questions if you want to optimize the likelihood that your organization retains its relevance over the long term. You need to make sure that you have people in your organization who ask such strange questions. And you must empower your organization to support people and processes that explore the seemingly abstract and strange. Of course, you can't really digitize a cup of coffee, but you can digitize the value that coffee creates. If you do not explore it further, others will, and they will be the ones who disrupt the metaphorical coffee with a very concrete meditation unit or a self-driving car.

NOTES

1. https://respace.dk/kontorpladser/coworking-spaces/hovedstaden/koebenhavn.
2. Frigyes Karinthy, Everything is Different, 1929.
3. https://en.wikipedia.org/wiki/Stanley_Milgram.
4. A term that was not actually used by Milgram, but was popularized by author John Guare in his play of the same name. https://en.wikipedia.org/wiki/John_Guare. Milgram's experiment has been criticized by some for not having been conducted with sufficient rigour, and people have questioned whether six links are the correct number. In the 2010s, the number has probably also fallen considerably by reason of the fact that there are around 2 billion people on Facebook that have created new connections. But regardless of the criticism, the principle behind the experiment serves as an example.
5. www.thync.com.
6. https://choosemuse.com.

PART II

UNDERSTAND THE IMMUNE SYSTEMS

Anything that is in the world when you're born is natural. Anything that's invented between when you're 15 and 35 is exciting. Anything invented after you're 35 is against the natural order of things.[1]

Douglas Adams

CHAPTER 6

IT'S THE EMPLOYEES THAT DON'T WANT TO: THE INDIVIDUAL IMMUNE SYSTEM

Some people bungee-jump. Others play whist. Some put all on red at the casino. Others prefer 5-year flexible house loans. Some start their own company. Others choose a job with the government. In other words, there is variation in the size of the risks we are willing to take.

A recent trial, conducted by a number of researchers from Stanford University and published in the recognized science journal *Nature*,[2] revealed a correlation between risk profiles and the brain's reward system. The researchers used rats in the experiment, because their brain structures are very similar to humans, and taught them to play a simple game with a potential reward. The rats were tasked with choosing which of two holes they would stick their snouts through to get sugar water. When they put their snouts through one hole, they were rewarded with a little bit of sugar water each time. When they put their snouts into the second hole, they were rewarded with a small amount of sugar water 75% of the time, and with a large amount of sugar water 25% of the time. Two-thirds of the rats consistently went for the stable option: the continuous small amount of sugar water. However, one-third of the rats had a higher risk profile and chose to go for the hole where they could potentially receive a greater amount of sugar water. The experiment showed that the most conservative rats – those that chose the hole with the continuous small amount of sugar water – had greater activity in the brain's nucleus accumbens, which is the part of the brain that plays an important role in motivation and reward, but also in addiction.[3] Activity was particularly detectable in the cells that produce type-2 dopamine receptors, also known as D2R. Dopamine is one of the brain's reward substances and can be addictive.

You might ask yourself why the rats didn't just choose the hole where they occasionally got a greater amount of sugar water, when they would, in any event, get sugar at this hole. This is because once the rats received a greater amount of sugar water followed by a smaller amount of sugar water at the same hole, they experienced this change as risky (the risk of not getting the greater amount of sugar water). However, the continuous small amount of sugar water in the first hole was stable and was therefore experienced as being less unsafe. This behaviour, also known as 'certainty effect',[4] also applies to humans. We prefer safe yields over likely yields. Even when the likely yields can be far better than the safe ones.

In light of these results, the researchers could then artificially stimulate the brain cells of the rats using optogenetic control,[5] a technique by which light can control genetically modified neurons in the brain that have been altered to be more light-sensitive. The researchers succeeded in stimulating the rats' brains using this method, thereby controlling their behaviour to be either less risk-averse, and to therefore opt for the larger but inconsistent amount of sugar water, or to be more risk-averse and, thus, go for the smaller but consistent amount of sugar water. The researchers also gave the rats pramipexole, a drug for Parkinson's disease, which is known to have the unfortunate (but relevant) side effect of turning human patients into notorious gamblers. The same happened in the rats. When they received the medication, they changed their behaviour and went for the more unsafe solution with the greater reward potential.

The experiment thus demonstrated that rats have different risk profiles, which depended on the chemical activity in their brains. As the rat brain is very similar to the human brain, the researchers concluded that one could probably also demonstrate and influence human risk preferences based on the chemical activities of the cells in the brain's nucleus accumbens.

Knowing this becomes interesting when dealing with the individual immune system's barriers to change and innovation. Because it shows that we as human beings have fundamentally different risk profiles, which is the first of three crucial parameters that defines the individual immune system. Human risk profiles are, among other things, controlled by the chemical activities of our brains, which make us more or less open to seeking out risk or stability. The majority of us are programmed, or 'wired' as brain researchers call it, to seek out stability and status quo. The minority seek out change and innovation.

You and your co-workers have undoubtedly done the DISC, Myers-Briggs or similar analyses to identify personal profiles in connection with things like recruitment. These analyses also show that we humans are different, but that we can be classified into specific groups. We have different degrees of extroversion, neuroticism (degree of worry), openness (towards the conventional vs. new), conscientiousness, and kindness.[6] There are no right or wrong traits. We are just different, and this plays a role in our daily actions at the workplace – not least in our actions when it comes to innovation projects or change processes. Some individuals also have special psychological barriers to major changes. These may be due to previous bad experiences or some of the built-in biases that we discussed in the chapter on massive transformative purposes.

Finally, the individual immune system is also guided by the capabilities of the employees. Do the employees actually have the right capabilities to participate in innovation projects or to join major organizational transformations? A study by PwC emphasizes how big the challenge is.[7] In a global survey of more than 2000 leaders from 56 countries, 76% stated that their employees either do not have, or do not acquire, the right capabilities to handle future corporate digitization. That figure is extremely high. If employees share the managers' experience – that they do not have the capabilities needed to undergo a digitization process – then this will, of course, cause barriers to that kind of change. If the organization moves from analogue to digital, where automations often cause employee duties to move higher up in the food chain, so to speak, and take on a higher degree of supervising, rather than operational, function as the algorithms take over this part of the work, this will obviously require new employee capabilities. This is one of the reasons why lifelong learning is becoming increasingly important at all levels. It is necessary to continuously develop employee capabilities as the world changes, and as the needs of the organization change. It sounds banal. But the analyses show that there is a long way for many companies to go before they act accordingly.

All three parameters of the individual immune system – personality profile, psychological barriers, and level of capabilities – are essential when a company evaluates how to overcome the barriers that stem from the individual immune system and to strengthen the organization's potential for innovation. It helps to understand your employees' personality profiles when you identify who to involve in various innovation projects; you need to design your way out of the psychological barriers that all human beings possess, something we will discuss more deeply in Chapter 11 when we discuss culture hacks; and you must ensure that you hire and train your employees to have the right capabilities. But, as an organization, you can't positively influence these parameters without also focusing on strengthening the organizational immune system's ability to absorb new things. In fact, this is even more important, as we will see in the next chapter.

NOTES

1. Mild revision of longer quote by Douglas Adams. https://www.business insider.com/douglas-adams-on-technology-2014-5?r=US&IR=T&IR=T
2. www.nature.com/articles/nature17400 and http://mentalfloss.com/article/77671/scientists-find-neurological-basis-risk-taking-trait.

3. https://en.wikipedia.org/wiki/Nucleus_accumbens.
4. www.jstor.org/stable/1914185?origin=crossref&seq=1#page_scan_tab_contents.
5. https://en.wikipedia.org/wiki/Optogenetics.
6. http://denstoredanske.dk/Krop,_psyke_og_sundhed/Psykologi/Psykologiske_termer/femfaktormodellen.
7. PwC 2017 Digital IQ Survey.

CHAPTER 7

'YOU GET WHAT YOU MEASURE': THE ORGANIZATIONAL IMMUNE SYSTEM

Change and innovation processes are complex. You don't succeed with change by making only one simple alteration or adjustment, and you often need to mobilize many people at the same time. So if the strategy calls for transformation, and you as a leader call for innovation, you need to ensure that the organizational immune system is strong enough to handle the job. Because if you don't strengthen the organizational immune system and address the barriers that you will otherwise be met with, then, from the individual employee's point of view, the rational behaviour will not necessarily be what is best for the organization. In game theory, this conflict is called a coordination problem.[1] All companies experience it. But here, too, you can design yourself out of the problems.

Maybe you've heard of the prisoner's dilemma, a classic way of illustrating coordination problems which was originally developed at the American research institute RAND in 1950[2] and subsequently further developed by Canadian mathematician Albert W. Tucker[3]. Two people are captured by the police and accused of a crime. The police do not have enough knowledge to convict them of the crime for which they've been arrested, but they know enough to imprison them for a minor offence. It is in the police's interest to make them testify against each other. Depending on how the prisoners choose to act with the police, they will go free, get a short prison sentence, or receive a long prison sentence. The prisoners have incomplete information about what's going on; they are isolated from each other so they cannot communicate; and they are deeply dependent on how the other captive acts. If both prisoners remain silent and do not testify against each other, they will both be sentenced to a year in prison. If only one of them testifies against the other while the other says nothing, the prisoner who testifies will go free and the prisoner who remains silent will get five years in prison. If both of them testify against each other, both will get three years in prison.

The biggest gain would, of course, be achieved by testifying against the other prisoner, so you can go free. That would therefore represent rational behaviour, from the individual's point of view. But as this is the case for both arrested parties, rational behaviour will lead them both to testify against each other and, thus, end up in jail for three years. The best behaviour, overall, is thus that they both remain silent, even if it leads to a year in prison. It is a classic coordination problem.

We see coordination problems unfold in many real situations: in the decision about whether or not to re- or disarm in an arms race between two nations; when the two leading cyclists in the Tour de France are lurking next to each other to see which one starts sprinting, and waiting for so long that they almost come to a standstill; in the passivity of all the world's countries in the face of climate problems; or when, in a given market, you don't know whether or not to continue to compete on price by continually lowering prices.

Think of the prisoner's dilemma, and replace the prison with your company and the prisoners with your employees (apologies for the imagery – there is, of course, no connection between your company and a prison!). Can you think of any situation where your organization would benefit from the cooperation of two departments, but where attempting this failed, either because each department experienced some form of 'penalty' for cooperating (through e.g. extra work, high costs, uncertainty about the result, or greater reward for the other party than for oneself), or because the departments, like the prisoners in the example, had incomplete information and, therefore, didn't have enough knowledge of the scope of the organization's needs, or of how big the reward could be? Analyses show that when it comes to change processes,[4] companies need to communicate ten times more than they generally do, so my guess is that you've answered 'yes'.

As a leader, you can actually promote the conduct required on behalf of the organization, but only if the system is adapted to the reality you want to create. If the system is not adapted to the goals, it doesn't matter how much you talk about wanting change; it's not going to happen. Therefore, there are three core parameters that the leader must ensure are consistent with the objectives of an organization's change, innovation, or development process, to avoid running into the coordination problems that inevitably arise if the individual's potential gains don't correspond with the organization's needs, thereby causing employees to lose their motivation.

– Key Performance Indicators (KPIs) and reward systems
– Legacy structures, processes, and tools
– Investors and shareholders.

KPIs AND REWARD SYSTEMS

In the fourth industrial[5] revolution which the world is just entering – where everything is digitized, tasks are automated, and routine jobs disappear in favour of more complex, creative positions – money only has a limited connection with performance.[6] Money is, of course, an important motivational factor for everyone, but whether you get 5, 10, or 20% more in the form of a bonus or reward has no direct proportional impact on performance, productivity, or the bottom line, as long as your pay is considered reasonable. A better strategy is to pay well from the outset to attract the best people, and then explore how to create jobs that are motivational in and of themselves[7] – regardless of salary. Or as Eric Schmidt, former CEO of Google, put it, 'Pay outrageously good people outrageously well, regardless of their title or tenure'[8] rather than giving performance-dependent bonuses and monetary rewards. Such arrangements can actually have the opposite effect to what is desired, and could cause less motivation and poorer results. In other words, modern people are increasingly motivated by intrinsic motivators like meaning, learning, and development, over extrinsic motivators like money, bonuses, and prestige.[9]

This also applies to idea generation and innovation. For example, a 10-year study conducted in Switzerland with more than 1400 companies showed that you don't get better ideas by rewarding employees with large sums of money for optimization suggestions than you do with lower sums. You get more ideas because more employees think it's smart to come up with ideas when they get money for it, but you get more bad ideas.[10] If you're going to give rewards, you need to reward the quality of the ideas.

Rewarding or punishing employees for their individual contributions to a process is not a given either, as it can make employees more risk-averse. They become afraid to make mistakes if it affects their salary or bonus, and therefore they hold back. We saw this very connection in a study done by Harvard professor J. Hoffer Gittell in an American airline. Airlines have traditionally cut employees' wages if they caused delays that were costly. Because the individual employee was penalized for making mistakes, it led to a culture where the employees were defensive, using their energy to cover their backs and blame others. It is not a culture that promotes cooperation or innovation. The survey led to a shift in focus from holding the individual employee accountable to making the whole team accountable, and the flight delays dropped significantly. Collaboration and results were optimized because of the switch from individual to team-based evaluation.[11]

In a world of increasing complexity, where technologies and industries are merging, as illustrated in the first few chapters, there is an increasing need for cooperation between people across competencies and across organizations. This means that the team's role becomes more important than the role of the individual. Therefore, you should increasingly be setting team-based goals over individual goals, ensuring that the entire team works in the same direction. There is also a much greater chance that the people on the ground know best what is needed to create and evaluate development. Nevertheless, KPIs are very often set from higher-ups in the organization without involving those who will realize these KPIs.

Intel, the American hardware giant that pioneered computer chip development, were also pioneers in the use of Objectives and Key Results (OKRs),[12] which offers a solution to the issues we've just discussed. OKRs differ from KPIs by being developed bottom-up in the organization, in collaboration with the employees themselves; being holistic so that they relate to the needs of the entire team and organization; and being both qualitative and quantitative.

The objectives are qualitative, e.g. 'We must internationalize', while key results are quantitative, e.g. 'We will enter at least two new markets this year'. The special thing about the way companies like Intel use OKRs is that the goals are made transparent to the entire organization so everyone can see each other's goals, even the CEO's. It increases the transparency of the organization and ensures that they work more towards the same overall goals. This also minimizes the risk that different departments have opposing goals – another classic situation that creates coordination problems. If, for instance, the sales department in a company is assessed on its ability to be customer-centric and to increasingly offer customized solutions, while the IT department is only assessed on its ability to reduce costs, this is likely to create a coordination problem. The two departments' goals are potentially opposed. The sales department can't help the customer to get more personalized solutions if IT only focuses on streamlining and reducing costs, and isn't rewarded for developing new solutions that can help the sales department offer more personalized solutions. If you work in a larger, established organization, you probably know that this is not just a hypothetical example. It happens all the time.

In my own company, we develop our OKRs in teams, so as not to have any individual goals (besides personal development goals); instead, we collaborate to meet the team's goals. We develop the goals together, share them with each other and make them accessible to all. It takes some time to integrate OKR processes, but it has a particularly positive effect on motivation, and it also increases individual insight into the organization's needs and cohesion.

As the examples above show, traditional measurement methods often do not work. The mindset behind most measurement and reward systems, and the mindset on which the majority of companies base their KPIs, originates from the industrial age and Frederick Taylor's scientific management theories, which are best exemplified by the principles behind Ford's assembly line factories. Here, people were doing monotonous jobs with predictable results, very little influence and a very high degree of supervision from higher-ups. But, in a modern society, the reality that this mindset reflects exists to a very limited extent. Therefore, if they want to realize their strategies, companies also need to change the tactics they apply to how they assess and reward their employees. Basically, modern people are motivated by feeling that their work is meaningful, through personal growth, by being praised and involved, by collaborating, and by having autonomy.[13] And this motivation creates results.

Instead of designing your measurement points based on a logic that assumes that there is always a direct connection between the measurement point and the end result ('we want to increase sales, so we only measure the number of units sold'), you should also develop your measurement points based on an indirect correlation between measurement points and end results. It could be a case of establishing measurement points for employee motivation for participating in projects and collaborating with customers, which has an indirect effect on sales and a positive impact on the culture.

The American Harvard professor Teresa Amabile's analyses of hundreds of teams show that people generally think that they will appear smarter in their bosses' eyes if they are critical.[14] An overwhelmingly critical mindset doesn't promote a culture of results. Criticism has its time and place, but it should not be the ground state. Especially not when we live in a world where companies have to constantly innovate and experiment, activities which require an openness that rarely prevails in companies. Therefore, the pharmaceutical company Johnson & Johnson specifically assesses their internal researchers for their awareness of what's happening within their field, regardless of whether it's in the research or business world, and rewards them equally regardless of whether the projects they launch are building on internally or externally developed ideas and research. They do so to avoid reflexive criticism and the 'not-invented-here' problem, which is often the first sign that criticism kills ideas in an early phase. Ideas and research should be evaluated solely on their potential and not on their origin.[15]

The big Danish water pump manufacturer Grundfos, which has established a new so-called digital factory that develops digital solutions across the organization (and that we will return to in Chapter 12), evaluates the digital factory's specially selected employees on how willing they are to help others and on the extent to which they are motivated to participate in the company's new digitization journey. The purpose is to ensure that all employees in the new unit, which plays a decisive role in bringing the whole organization forward, become aware of and work in the best way to make the right products and build the right culture in the organization.

Microsoft, known to be an extremely competitive sales-focused organization, has done something similar in the transformation process that the organization has been in since the new CEO, Satya Nadella, took the reins in 2015 to make the culture less competitive and more focused on customers and collaboration. Although employees are still assessed on revenue, they are now also assessed on their ability to create solutions with customers as well as whether they share and build on the knowledge of others.

In Alphabet's (Google's parent company) experimental laboratory X, there are even rewards for the teams that kill ideas and shut down projects when employees discover insoluble problems over the course of the experiments. It may sound strange to reward people for not carrying out projects, but there is a method in the madness that references what psychologists call the sunk cost fallacy or, in other words, the point at which you have invested so much time, money, or emotion in a project that you can no longer make yourself stop. Rewarding employees for killing ideas and closing down projects avoids the problem of people becoming too emotionally involved in their projects and keeping them alive for longer than is healthy. This not only saves employees and organizations time, but also reduces development costs and increases motivation.[16] Also note that it is the team, and not individuals, that is rewarded and makes the decision to shut something down.

In a survey conducted by *MIT Sloan Management Review* and Google in January 2018, more than 3000 leaders from around the world were asked about their KPI strategies. Conclusion number one was that there seems to be no best practice when it comes to KPIs. Conclusion number two was that KPIs rarely guide the organization. This is, of course, paradoxical, seeing that the entire purpose of KPIs is to be a management tool. But as much as 30% of the leaders felt that KPIs had a limited effect on how they lead people and processes, and only 26% agreed that their functional KPIs were consistent with the organization's strategic goals. In other words: there is room for improvement for when organizations work on their goals. What the study also showed, on the other hand, was that there was a huge difference in the return of KPI efforts for organizations that used KPIs alone to monitor employee performance and for those organizations that used KPIs to help employees strengthen their performance.

Goodhart's law states that any observable statistical rule tends to collapse when it is used for the purposes of controlling outcomes.[17] A more direct way to express it is that as soon as you turn a focus area into a measurement point, it loses its value because people, deliberately or subconsciously, start using their energy to meet the measurement point in the short term, regardless of whether or not the long-term implications may be poor.[18] As always, when it comes to innovation, development, change, and culture, there are no simple solutions. However, an inclusive process where measurement points are consistent with the strategy across departments, and which focuses on team, mindset, and culture, is crucial for organizations to be innovative and to get what they measure.

LEGACY STRUCTURES, PROCESSES, AND TOOLS

KPIs and reward systems are part of a company's structures, and, together with IT and production systems as well as governance and working methods, they constitute a complex system.

As pointed out earlier, in the vast majority of cases, people don't control the systems; the systems control people. Sometimes, we see that societal systems are forced to change due to pressure from the population. In peaceful situations, it is called democracy when the population votes in new powers, and in turbulent times it is called revolution. But it is different for companies. Here we do not see revolutions orchestrated by the employees. There may be protests, which we have begun to see more and often for moral reasons, especially in the United States, where employees at Google, Facebook, and Salesforce have protested against their companies' cooperation with Trump's government. In some cases, it has caused change and, as an example, Google has introduced a new ethical set of rules in relation to cooperation with military units.[19] If the pressure from employees is high enough, it may lead to changes in management and behaviour. But companies are not democracies, and employees only have limited power.

As a leader, you need to be very aware of the system's power over the results. Just because the systems are not being challenged by the employees does not mean that the employees think that the systems are appropriate. Employees are more likely to resign themselves to accepting the limitations of the systems even if they don't feel they're appropriate. Or the employees simply find something else to do. Regardless of the strategy you apply as a leader, or the measurement points you choose, and the stories you tell, you will not achieve the desired results if you do not develop the system for the future you want to create.

Anyone with just a little bit of experience with older organizations knows that legacy IT and production facilities often cause problems. They've built their products and services on IT systems and machines that may well have been cutting edge when they started their successful business. However, as development accelerates, the systems quickly become obsolete and it becomes harder and harder to optimize and maintain their innovation power and competitiveness. Nevertheless, upgrades are delayed, probably for far too long, because the cost of changing systems is huge, and sometimes the switch is even impossible as the entire company's business case relies on these systems. We even hear companies that are less than ten years old (some would still call them startups) which have been successful and scaled up, stating that their biggest difficulties have been legacy IT.

I'm probably not the only one who has experienced situations like the following. An employee has a great idea about how the company can develop a new service that could potentially open up new target groups to the company. The employee shares their enthusiasm with the boss, who can understand the opportunity, but also spots some potential difficulties, and therefore says the paradoxical words: 'Great idea. We must do that. But could you just run it past Legal?' THUMP. You can almost hear the idea, motivation, and potential fall to the ground with a bang. Because the moment anything is run past Legal, all potential reasons why something cannot be done are rooted out in extraordinarily lengthy processes. Sorry, Legal! It is not your fault. You are just doing your job. And you are important. But the question is whether an idea has to be run past Legal. Of course, you must follow the law, but sometimes you should hold off involving the company's support functions until you have something very concrete and considered to ask. Occasionally, you should also consider whether the new initiatives or ideas should be fitted into traditional structures. We see more and more banks breaking with that principle – without breaking the law or acting unethically. They start, buy, or invest in the fintech companies which – because they are not banks – can operate by a different set of rules, thus exploring more potential than is possible in the banking world.

The manager's response to the innovative employee could also have been: 'Super idea. We must do that. We just need to make sure it's compatible with IT.' THUMP. Again. Yes, maybe it should be compatible with IT, but maybe it shouldn't. Maybe the idea should be developed outside existing structures. It depends on how closely the idea lies to the company's core services, and the extent to which the company already has the technological and human skills to develop the idea. We will return to this in the third part of the book, where we look at how companies need to innovate along multiple tracks at the same time.

A third scenario could be that the boss approves the idea, and then asks the employee to initiate a traditional waterfall process and commence the usual requirements specifications that, in the best case scenario, would entail a 24-month development horizon. The problem here is that this introduces the risk that an unknown and invisible startup could be down in a basement somewhere developing exactly the same idea – just in a much more agile and speedy way. Probably prototyping their way to a solution that would allow them to launch a minimum viable product (MVP) within six months – and without first needing to prepare a business case, because their KPIs are about users and not about revenue and earnings. Such details are only discussed by many entrepreneurs at a later date. That approach may seem both arrogant and stupid. And, it may well be. The failure rates for startups are enormous, and the most common reason why startups fail is that there aren't enough people that want to own their products. However, if you have investments backing you, it can be freeing to reduce your fear of error and act more experimentally without having to prepare business models before launching a new product.

Legacy structures, processes, and tools create control, overview, and security in organizations. But they are also time-consuming, costly, and innovation-limiting. The faster that technological advancement progresses and the more accessible technology becomes, the more of a problem companies' heaviness and slowness will become and the more important the need to reconsider their methods becomes. You also need investors and shareholders to be on board with this. And herein lies the third parameter that weakens the organizational immune system.

INVESTORS AND SHAREHOLDERS

In 2018, the streaming service Netflix designated $12–13 billion for the development and production of new shows and films.[20] That's twice as much as they spent in 2017, about three times as much as the nationwide US television channel CBS spends, and five times as much as what was spent by HBO, which has given us cultural gifts like *The Sopranos, Game of Thrones,* and *Westworld.*[21] Netflix can handle this budget because their investors don't expect to make money in the short term. Let me repeat that: the investors do not expect to earn money in the short term. And that's great, because Netflix loses a lot of money. By 2017, the amount was close to 2 billion dollars.[22]

The investors, of course, expect to recover their investments. And they also expect to multiply their investments over time. But they think long-term. Therefore, Netflix is focused more on getting more users than on being in the black. And things look good on this front, because Netflix added more than 23 million subscribers in 2017, bringing them up to over 100 million users worldwide.

And Netflix's ambitions are extremely big. The CEO, Reed Hastings, is known to have said that Netflix's biggest competitor is sleep.[23] To be honest, I'm not sure how I feel about that message. It is well-documented that sleep is extremely important for people's quality of life and health. If Netflix really wants to exchange their customers' sleep with more binge-watching, then I can see some ethical issues with that business model. And I say this as a major consumer of their product. A sleepy major consumer. But maybe Hastings made that comment tongue-in-cheek. Nevertheless, very few companies have the privilege of having investors and shareholders who are willing to see losses month after month, year after year. Companies are typically penalized as soon as they don't earn money and meet the needs of shareholders and investors for security. But in Netflix's case, and in the case of other fast-scaling companies like Amazon, Spotify, Tesla, WeWork, etc., investors and shareholders have been taught to prioritize growth over earnings.

As a CEO or a senior executive of a legacy organization, you probably can't convince your investors and shareholders to think like that. You are probably not even interested in doing so. But what you should be interested in is teaching your investors and shareholders to think beyond the next couple of quarters – to take the long view. Because Amazon is in it for the long haul. Tesla is in it for the long haul. Japan's Softbank is in it for the long haul. The Vision Fund, Softbank's investment company, which has raised an incredible $100 billion,[24] and, at the time of writing this, is said to be raising another 100-billion-dollar fund, has a 300-year time horizon.[25]

As a legacy organization, you don't have to think 300 years into the future – that is an extremely long time, and no one has the slightest clue what the world will look like in 300 years. But you should think 30 years into the future and find out how your company can do experiments today that optimize your potential to play an important role in the world in 2050. Such a vision of the future requires you to have your investors and shareholders on board. That they understand the need for innovation and change, and this is often difficult for larger, established organizations. Fortunately, the picture is starting to look a bit different. More and more legacy companies – especially in the automotive industry, which has been hard pressed since the financial crisis, while also experiencing brand new standards set by companies such as Tesla in electric cars and Google in self-driving cars – are experiencing investors who are starting to require that the car manufacturers initiate disruption initiatives because the investors have realized that the status quo is the riskiest state.

So, where we have previously seen companies being punished by their investors and shareholders and limited by their boards for wanting to invest too much in innovation and strategic initiatives that deviate from the traditional core focus, we are starting to see the opposite. At the time of writing, Ford Motors had just announced that they are investing a huge billion-dollar amount to digitize the entire organization. This immediately resulted in a rising share price. As we will see later, Ford is investing in both augmenting and mutating innovation, i.e. by both upgrading and challenging their core. Toyota and Daimler are doing something similar, and Denmark's logistics giant Maersk has initiated a large number of initiatives, where they both digitize the core business and experiment with new blockchain platforms outside of the core.

In the pharmaceutical industry, the price of developing a drug approved by the US Food and Drug Administration (FDA) doubled 13 times between 1975 and 2005.[26] So where the software world talks about Moore's law – that the price/performance of computing power doubles about every eighteenth month, a decisive driving force for software companies' innovative power – the pharmaceutical industry has begun to talk about Eroom's law, which the attentive reader will notice is just Moore spelled backwards, because innovation costs rise so sharply that there is a risk of a reverse Moore law. This development is putting pressure on the industry, which must increasingly consider how to stop this negative spiral. Energy companies worldwide are selling off their legacy businesses and focusing on sustainable energy solutions instead. Both Danish Ørsted (formerly DONG Energy) and Norwegian Equinor (formerly Statoil) are even changing their names to communicate to the outside world that these are new times.

Most innovation initiatives are initiated by necessity. The core business is threatened, and the threats are so dramatic that many companies fear for their lives. But it doesn't have to get that far. You shouldn't wait for the problems to become enormous before upgrading your innovation ambitions. On the contrary, you should act while things are going well and while you have the resources to future-proof your organization's existence. Therefore, you need to understand your organizational immune system so that you can design your way around the barriers embedded within your legacy structures, processes, and systems; so that you can steer your KPIs and reward systems towards a new reality; and so that you can motivate your investors and shareholders to understand the need to move away from the status quo. Finally, you must also address the societal immune system. Because there is also an immune system outside the company's own domain that directly affects its innovation power.

NOTES

1. www.oecd.org/cfe/regional-policy/presentation_coordination_failures_a_game_theoretic_approach.pdf.
2. https://en.wikipedia.org/wiki/Prisoner%27s_dilemma & William Poundstone - Prisoner's Dilemma, 1999.
3. https://en.wikipedia.org/wiki/Albert_W._Tucker.
4. www.forbes.com/sites/johnkotter/2011/06/14/think-youre-communicating-enough-think-again/#5e7dc1a76275.
5. Klaus Schwab, The Fourth Industrial Revolution, 2017.
6. Bruno S Frey and Margit Osterloh, Successful Management by Motivation, 2002.

7. Bruno S Frey and Margit Osterloh, Successful Management by Motivation, 2002.
8. Eric Schmidt, How Google Works, 2015.
9. www.princeton.edu/~rbenabou/papers/RES2003.pdf.
10. Bruno S Frey and Margit Osterloh, Successful Management by Motivation, 2002.
11. J Hoffer Gittell, Anomali of High Performance: Reframing Economic and Organizational Theory of Performance Management, 1999.
12. John Doerr, Measure What Matters: OKRs, 2018.
13. Bruno S Frey and Margit Osterloh, Successful Management by Motivation, 2002.
14. https://hbr.org/1998/09/how-to-kill-creativity.
15. Boston Consulting Group, The Most Innovative Companies 2016. www.bcg.com/d/press/12january2017-most-innovative-companies-2016-142287.
16. www.fastcompany.com/3058866/how-googles-moonshot-x-division-helps-its-employees-embrace-failure.
17. https://en.wikipedia.org/wiki/Goodhart%27s_law.
18. Jerry Z. Muller, The Tyranny of Metrics, 2018.
19. www.theverge.com/2018/5/30/17408446/google-ai-guidelines-weaponry-military-pentagon-maven-contract.
20. www.investopedia.com/news/netflix-spend-13b-original-content-2018.
21. http://fortune.com/2018/07/08/netflix-original-programming-13-billion.
22. https://empresa-journal.com/2017/12/30/can-netflix-ever-make-money.
23. www.fastcompany.com/40491939/netflix-ceo-reed-hastings-sleep-is-our-competition.
24. www.softbank-ia.com/vision-fund.
25. https://journal.accj.or.jp/masayoshi-sons-300-year-plan/.
26. Fredrik Erixon and Björn Weigel, The Innovation Illusion, 2016.

CHAPTER 8

WE DON'T KNOW IT, SO WE DON'T WANT IT: THE SOCIETAL IMMUNE SYSTEM

As is the case with the individual and organizational immune system, there are three key parameters in the societal immune system that you must address if you want to strengthen your innovative power. These are:

Legislation

Legacy customers and suppliers

The general economic climate.

LEGISLATION

In GE's annual global innovation barometer, 68% of respondents in 2018 indicated that their governments were unable to regulate innovation because they couldn't keep up with the pace of innovation.[1] Respondents in the study experienced this whether or not they were for or against higher degrees of protectionism. The report's conclusion was that innovation is driven by the private sector, and the legislative power can't keep up.

One of the most obvious examples of this is the war between Uber and the taxi companies around the world. Whether in Denmark, Sweden, France, Germany, England, the United States, India, or China, there has been a fight, and even physical combat, between the established taxi companies and Uber's taxi-like service. In the vast majority of countries, if you are a taxi driver, you live under strict regulation. Becoming a taxi driver is by no means easy. There are limits to the number of licenses issued for driving a taxi, and in New York, for example, you must have a so-called taxi medallion, which is very expensive.[2] The barriers to becoming a taxi driver, or for a haulier to add a taxi to their portfolio, are therefore very high.

In 2009, Uber started as a limousine service in San Francisco, but soon added a more accessible mainstream service where individuals could book other individuals to drive them from point A to point B via Uber's digital platform and app at a much-reduced price. Thanks to digitization, you could use new service standards to book the car digitally, see how long the wait is, and pay automatically through the Uber app. The Uber drivers drive according to digital navigation apps, e.g. Google Maps or Waze, so the route is always automatically encrypted, meaning that you as a passenger don't have to worry about whether or not the driver has chosen the most direct route, or if they can find the way.

Uber has generally been well-received by customers. The low prices, coupled with the digitization of the service, have raised the level of transport convenience and have made Uber such a logical choice for many people that it has in record time grown from being an insignificant startup to becoming one of the world's most valuable unicorns with a market value of $68 billion.[3]

The low prices and the ability to scale the fleet so efficiently was possible primarily because Uber's business model is thoroughly digitized, it uses private individuals as drivers (whom they additionally haven't directly employed, to avoid a number of regulatory and fiscal demands), and drivers use their own cars. This means that Uber's marginal cost of adding a car to the fleet is close to zero. Compared to the taxis companies' traditionally analogue service, higher prices, higher costs for adding an additional car to the fleet (taxi medallion or license, the cost of the car, and the cost of making the car fit for purpose), the two modes of transportation are fighting a completely uneven fight. Taxis simply cannot beat Uber's business model unless legislators support them.

However, Uber's appearance around the world has also been characterized by a very aggressive strategy, which, in many cases, has ignored existing legislation and has apparently been operating on a philosophy of 'better to ask for forgiveness than for permission'. In many cases, they've simply moved into a city, recruited drivers and started the service without getting the necessary permits to do so. Understandably, the established taxi companies have been upset about this. Since Uber does not operate with drivers in the same technical sense as taxi companies do, and therefore do not feel that they need to comply with taxi legislation, they have also avoided the many rules that local taxi companies must comply with. The taxi companies have experienced Uber's presence as unfair competition and have protested strongly. We've seen taxi strikes in many places around the world. In Paris, there have been fierce physical fights, car vandalizations and almost warlike conditions. To alert the authorities to their dissatisfaction with the many Uber cars, taxi drivers blocked Barcelona airport in the summer of 2018 so Uber could not operate in the middle of the holiday season, and thousands of people had trouble getting home from vacation. And in many countries, the established taxi companies have – with good effect – mounted a massive lobbying campaign to put pressure on politicians. After negotiations with the authorities in Denmark, Uber pulled out of Copenhagen and Aarhus because they couldn't reach an agreement on Uber's terms. In Sweden, agreements have been entered into in which only taxi drivers are authorized to drive for Uber. In many cities, the authorities have imposed tight restrictions on how many Uber cars are allowed to drive in the city to restrict competition against the taxi companies.

Viewed from the outside, and without siding with either Uber or the taxi companies, the conflict between the two is a good new example of a classic problem: the societal immune system comes into force when new business models pop up and gain so much popularity that they become mainstream. The challenger – in this case Uber – circumvented the law through their new business model, by defining themselves as something that differs from a taxi company, even though it was actually offering the same service. They circumvented tax and employment legislation by not hiring, but setting up freelance contracts with their drivers. Nobody had done anything like this before on this scale, and because Uber gained so much popularity, the initiative was a shock to both the taxi companies and the authorities. There was simply no preparedness for anything like Uber.

Initially, Uber was ignored, but as they grew larger and more economically significant, this strategy proved untenable. Therefore, the established actors launched lobbying efforts while the authorities introduced new legislation in an effort to maintain the status quo. In many cases, authorities find it more important to maintain the status quo – in this case, this meant ensuring that the taxi companies could maintain their business model, and maintaining the existing laws and processes in a somewhat unchanged form – than to listen to the wishes of the customers and open up for competition by modernizing the legislation.

Many will probably accuse me of siding too much with Uber and ignoring the fact that Uber has broken the law on many counts. But this is by no means my intention: I'm not looking to defend Uber. Their aggressiveness has been too fierce. They have ignored the law and have, in many cases, acted in a morally reprehensible way. I consider myself to be a lawful citizen who cannot accept anyone deliberately breaking the law to do business. But Uber's entry into the world has shown some obvious opportunities for modernizing some very obsolete transportation services and corresponding legislation. Taxi companies around the world have been caught unawares. They had never previously experienced any noteworthy competition, and they had therefore not modernized their services. And the authorities have maintained legislation that, in a modern digitized world, seems antiquated and unconstructive for customers, taxi companies, and new entrants alike.

The Uber case has progressed in peaks and troughs. The first wave was Uber's aggressive entry. The second wave was the taxi companies' defence through striking and lobbyism, and the third wave is the current attempt at adaptation, where legislation in certain places, e.g. in Denmark, is being modernized to a certain extent,[4] and Uber is adjusting its business model and behaviour accordingly, or choosing to withdraw. Barcelona has restricted the number of licenses issued to Uber drivers.[5] In New York, the authorities have decided to temporarily stop the number of licenses being issued to Uber and other car sharing companies such as Lyft to 'investigate the actors' impact on the city',[6] and to introduce a minimum wage for drivers, which they were previously not receiving because they acted as freelancers and not employees. Unions are also dissatisfied with this initiative, as they have an understandable concern about whether or not existing legislation sufficiently protects people working for companies that act as so-called gig economy companies, like Uber and Lyft.

The struggle between the old and new business models, where the weapons of choice are lobbyism and legislation, is by no means new. Back in 1865, car legislation was introduced in England under which all cars were only allowed to drive four kilometres an hour in cities and had to have a person walking in front of the driving car with a red flag to warn the surroundings about the new vehicle.[7] This law was, however, repealed after about 20 years. In the 1970s and 1980s, there was a ban on setting up satellite dishes in Denmark, to protect the Danish television monopoly of the time. The law only changed thanks to civil disobedience. In Sweden, there was a ban on cordless phones in the 1980s to protect the monopoly's fixed-line solutions.[8] In 1990, the Danish dairy giant MD Foods broke the law by launching the butter blend product Kærgården, as it was illegal to mix plant oil and butter into one product. Shortly after the ban was lifted, Kærgården became the country's best-selling butter product.[9] Since its foundation, Tesla has encountered great opposition to their sales strategy in the United States, where they have established their own sales channels in branded stores and online sales and thus eliminated the intermediary layer, i.e. the car dealer. In order to protect car dealers, direct sales of cars by the manufacturer are prohibited in several US states.[10] The cryptocurrency Bitcoin, especially known for its enormous increase in value by over 7.5 million percent since its creation in 2009, and for its huge fluctuations in value, is illegal in 11 countries.

To begin with, the societal immune system is almost always the strongest, which, in many ways, is positive. As is the case with the Uber matter, critical issues are considered, such as human working conditions and the long-term socioeconomic effect of the case. However, the immune system continues to show its weaknesses through its lack of flexibility; its lack of regular analyses of advantages and disadvantages for customers, citizens, and the level of competition; its difficulty with adapting to new circumstances; and perhaps, most of all, the lack of preparedness to handle entirely new models. We will only see this more as technological development creates new opportunities and opens up new business models.

The societal immune system is almost always a friend of the well-established, traditional company. Because it usually contributes to keeping new entrants out of the market. The more regulated a market is, the harder it is for new actors to enter. However, as the Uber case shows, the societal immune system can also easily become a cushion for traditional companies, ultimately helping to limit the company's innovative power. As mentioned earlier, the financial sector is experiencing this in the form of pressure from fintech companies that can act in ways that banks are legally prohibited from acting, simply because they aren't classified as banks. The former monopoly postal service PostNord is required by law to service all Danes – including those in the outermost regions – with frequent mail delivery, despite the fact that we live in a world where, in a country like Denmark, the physical letter has long lost its role as the fastest written communication medium, and this costly obligation, thus, seems unnecessary. Hence, this obligation serves as an important example of how the societal immune system, as exemplified by legislation, unnecessarily restricts a company. In their book *The Innovation Illusion*, Erixon and Weigel even argue that things are headed in the wrong direction, and that regulation has been steadily tightening since the 1980s and 1990s,[11] which negatively impacts the country's innovation power.

We live in a world where we need to get used to drones as a way of transporting packages, pizzas, and medicine; autonomous vehicles as means of transportation for people; biological tools like CRISPR-Cas9 that can modify genes in plants, animals, and humans; solar cell prices and battery capacities that produce solar energy cheaper than fossil fuels; and artificial intelligence that leads to automations, which means that more and more decisions, hitherto made by conscious human beings, are now being made by machines – in many cases without people knowing. In the vast majority of cases, our society is not geared to address these developments. But we cannot afford, either economically or humanely, to let the societal immune system make us so reactive. Development is going too fast, and the implications are too big for this kind of reactivity. Just think of the environmental problems which we are doing too little about. We need to figure out how barriers in the societal immune system can be eliminated so that we can be at the forefront of developments, including through proactive legislation. Not by predicting all the implications, because this is impossible, but by initiating informed debates and permitting experimentation so that we can explore the new in order to uncover how best we can all benefit – that goes for the companies that introduce the technologies and business models, but more importantly, that also goes for the people, the citizens, who will be using them and drawing value from them.

If we don't actively do anything, the new business models will seek out places where there are no restrictions. On the African continent, for instance, we are seeing many countries 'leapfrogging', i.e. skipping technological generations. In Kenya, mobile payments have become crucial to the country's socioeconomic state. They have not been limited by legacy IT, like the copper in the ground which has been crucial for the creation of landline telephony in the Western world. They have gone straight to mobile technology, and are now in a leading position in comparison to many other parts of the world. Tanzania is a leader in the use of decentralized solar energy, where villages, and even the individual homes, become their own power plant, as it's been expressed by Asger Trier Bing, CEO of M-Payg, a company that develops battery-powered, mobile-paid solar solutions for African private consumers. It is a model that challenges the Western tradition of centralized energy distribution, and which will ultimately mean free energy for the user.

A gain from greater openness to new technologies and business models is that the companies that develop the new technologies and experiment with them, will move them where the will for experimentation is the greatest. For example, countries such as South Africa and Rwanda have the most liberal drone laws in the world. They do because they have very little infrastructure in terms of roads and transport options. They desperately need alternatives so that they can get food and medicine to their citizens who are at risk of isolation during the rainy season. But this also means that Rwanda may become the world's leading expert in drone technology – not Sweden, Germany, or the United States. It gives Rwanda huge first-mover opportunities to build their finances around drone technology, and also allows them to take the lead in developing the ethical standards for drone use throughout the rest of the world.

It is worth considering, for instance, whether we want to introduce the most prohibitive legislation possible in the development of gene editing technologies and artificial intelligence, perhaps even completely banning research, like the Americans did with stem cell research under George W. Bush, thus disengaging completely from developing and influencing it. Or do we want to work on tailoring legislation that makes it attractive for companies to develop and collaborate with academia to develop opportunities and, through this learning process, to also define the legislative and ethical frameworks for what we want and what we don't want? As always, there are no easy solutions.

But that does not lessen the need for these discussions. And the big, established organizations have huge opportunities to set this important agenda and to benefit from this proactivity. If they dare.

LEGACY CUSTOMERS AND SUPPLIERS

By nature, very few people are innovators or first movers. According to Everett Rogers' classic model of how innovations spread, only 2.5% of us are innovators. They are the ones who buy the new products even when they don't work, simply because they are excited about the technologies in and of themselves. Then there are the very early users (13.5%) who jump on the bandwagon as soon as the first few hiccups have passed. Approximately one third constitutes the early majority, one third is the late majority, and approximately 16% are laggards, i.e. those who adopt a technology or innovation when it simply becomes impossible not to. In his influential book *Crossing the Chasm*, Geoffrey Moore analyses how the vast majority of products and services fail to make the leap between appealing to the first two groups, often collectively called first movers, to the early mainstream users. Hence the name of the book. How do you avoid falling into the abyss and create a service that has mainstream appeal? As is the case with customers, the minority of suppliers are first movers and, thereby, first to follow the trend when it seems obvious that they have to.

If you, as a large, well-established company, or as part of the public sector for that matter, want to set the standard and future-proof your organization, you need to educate your customers and suppliers and help them enter the future you want to create.

Anders Mortensen, a Google director who is in charge of their digital agency partners in North America – whom we often visit when we take groups to Silicon Valley to get behind the scenes of the most innovative companies and ecosystems – likes asking the following question: 'If a person using Google's search engine can't spell a particular product name, whose responsibility is that?' Google believes it is Google's responsibility. Even though there is a school system that is responsible for teaching citizens how to read and write, and even though producers are responsible for raising awareness about their own products, it is ultimately also Google's responsibility. Because if the user can't find the solution that he/she needs, Google is not living up to its responsibility as a search engine, but is minimizing the impact they can exert on behalf of the direct customers who buy advertising space from them. Where most companies take responsibility for the customer in the first degree, i.e. when the customer interacts directly with them, Google also takes responsibility for the customer in the second and third degree, because they know that this effort has a derivative effect on their own results. That's why, for example, there are automated suggestions when you type something in the search box on the

Google Search Engine, and why Google runs courses to teach their direct customers to be better at sales.

Why do consultancies like Accenture, PwC, and Deloitte spend millions of dollars running courses and workshops for their customers about new technologies, even though they don't develop and sell these technologies themselves? Because they help customers develop their business by giving them a greater understanding of technology, which is a prerequisite for laying and executing the right strategies. For the same reason, the software company SAP and the technology company Ericsson establish big, stunning customer experience centres and maker spaces (with 3D-printers, CNC milling machines and other modern tools) around the world where they facilitate prototyping workshops and hackathons for their customers. They help their customers develop their businesses by understanding and experimenting with their potentials. Of course, with the intention of including SAP and Ericsson's own products as part of the solutions. But they take a much broader responsibility than that of narrowly focusing on their own products.

That's why water pump producer Grundfos operates with SWAT teams, for example, which they send out with their sales teams to customers and end users. Their task is to teach customers and end users how to use Grundfos products and digital solutions and how these solutions can be customized to suit the customers' own businesses and goals concerning, e.g. uptime and reduced energy consumption.

Denmark consists of 99% small and medium-sized enterprises[12] (SMEs); the same is basically true in countries such as Sweden, Germany, and the USA. The biggest long-term challenges facing SMEs are their lack of innovation power, lack of awareness about the need for digitization and innovation, and lack of resources. These companies often have enough on their plates with staying on track and delivering their core services. They do not have Grundfos, SAP, or Google's innovation power and cannot keep up with their pace. If SMEs are an important part of these businesses' value chains, then they need to also help the SMEs upgrade their core so that they can cross the chasm that Geoffrey Moore describes, allowing customers to use their products. The companies that take responsibility for their customers' problems are the companies that will win the market.

THE ECONOMIC CLIMATE

The technology company IBM was founded in 1911 as a result of a merger of three different technology companies, all of which began during the long depression of 1873–1896.[13] Hewlett-Packard was founded in 1935 in the aftermath of the Great Depression in the United States, and Apple launched the iPod in October 2001, just after the dot-com bubble burst.[14] Richard Florida, who is famous for defining the creative class, has described the 2008 financial crisis as a 'reset'[15] because he, using the Austrian economist Schumpeter's terminology,[16] experiences crises as opportunities for creative destruction, in which the old is broken down to build the new. And there is also no doubt that crises allow for a reconsideration of what currently exists, not least for the most entrepreneurial people. There is also no doubt that crises lead to replacements of who is the leading player. According to McKinsey, the aftermath of the 2001 crisis saw a replacement of 15% of the leading companies across industries in the United States.[17] But macroeconomically, crises are not good for innovation. According to a report from the OECD, the 2008 financial crisis significantly impeded the global innovation force. Over 25% of European companies reduced their innovation budgets; in South America, every fourth company stopped their ongoing development projects; and the leading organizations in research and development spending reduced their budgets by 1.9% in 2009. England's total research and development expenditure fell from index 99 to 93 between 2008 and 2010, Sweden's fell from index 110 to 95, while Denmark's remained fairly unchanged from 110 to 109. However, things went differently in China, where research and development investments almost exploded from index 117 to 170, and a number of other countries that we do not traditionally compare ourselves with – like Estonia, Hungary, Korea, and Poland – also increased their research and development activity in the same period.[18]

The report also shows, to no one's surprise, that the small and medium-sized enterprises suffered most in the first few years after the financial crisis occurred. Whereas the large companies generally had financial resources that they could allocate to other parts of the organization as sales fell, thus limiting cuts on innovation and investment, SMEs were far more fragile and forced to reduce their activities.[19]

I remember being a young, relatively new graduate, working as a project manager at a small research institute, while the dot-com crisis in 2001 was exacerbated by the indescribable terrorist attack at the World Trade Center in New York. The world was in shock and sales in our company stopped almost immediately. Budgets for existing projects were reduced and the pipeline was emptied as our customers stopped almost all activity. The same thing happened when the financial crisis occurred in 2008, while I was working as a manager at another larger research company. At the end of 2008, I remember we naively said that we would not put up with the financial crisis influencing our company that had been experiencing tremendous growth before then. But it did influence the company, and once again, all activity from our customers dropped significantly. We therefore scaled down all our costs to a minimum and did what we could to increase sales elsewhere. Most of all, though, we just hoped for the best.

At the same time, my co-founder Laila Pawlak received a Central Company Registration number for her first company DARE2. In the summer of 2009, I joined the company, which we developed to become a leader in experience economy and consulting in the creation of customer experiences. Today, everyone talks about experiences in a business context as if it were a natural thing to do, but I have to say that this wasn't the case in 2009. We were fortunate enough to work with the very best in the field. Among others, Joe Pine, co-author of the book *The Experience Economy,* which defined this important subject field, became a close friend, mentor, and collaborator to us. *The Experience Economy* was a blue ocean in the advisory world at that time. Many companies were sceptical and risk-averse and did not want to talk to us at all. A typical response was: 'What are we going to do with experiences? We are not Disney World.' But some people saw the possibilities in adjusting their perspectives on how to engage their customers and to innovate by looking more holistically at their opportunities for value creation. This openness was obviously motivated by the fact that the business world was in crisis. But it enabled us to benefit from the creative destruction that Schumpeter talked about. 'One man's trash, another man's treasure'? There's obviously something to it. Crises create new opportunities, but it is important to know, and learn from history, that the very fewest are strengthened by crises. At least in the short run. The economic climate is the subparameter of the three immune systems in which companies personally exert the least control. But again, innovation proves to be the red thread in how to successfully navigate through crises and get to the other side unscathed.

The Three Immune Systems: Individual, Organization, Society

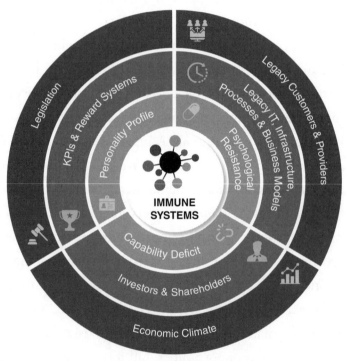

Model 2 The three immune systems that affect organizations' innovation power.
Source: Kris Østergaard

We have now discussed the three immune systems that a company needs to understand in order to create the best possible foundation for the innovation strategy that we will unveil in the third and last part of the book. Just as the body's biological immune system is crucial to human health, the individual, organizational, and societal immune systems are important mechanisms for us as employees, as companies, and as societies. They protect us, but they also limit us, and in a rapidly evolving world accelerated by technological achievements, a business leader has to analyse the various parameters that make up each of the three immune systems in order to maximize their organization's innovative power.

It is essential to understand that the immune system is not just about people's lack of willingness to change. Of course, there is a resistance to change in us human beings, depending on our personality profiles, psychological barriers, and capability sets, and a leader needs to take this seriously. But the challenges encountered in creating successful transformation and development projects are far more systemic than they are human. The system almost always beats the person, especially in organizations, so organizations need to adapt their KPIs and reward systems, legacy structures, processes, and tools, as well as their investor and shareholder initiatives to optimize the likelihood of success. Finally, there is the societal immune system, which includes legislation, legacy customers and suppliers, and the economic climate. It is the layer over which an organization has the least control, but one that it nevertheless needs to proactively address.

NOTES

1. https://s3.amazonaws.com/dsg.files.app.content.prod/gereports /wp-content/uploads/2018/02/12141110/GE_Global_Innovation_ Barometer_2018-Full_Report.pdf.
2. https://ny.curbed.com/2018/6/11/17450366/nyc-taxi-medallions-bankruptcy-auction.
3. www.cbinsights.com/research/unicorn-startup-market-map/.
4. http://taxilov.dk.
5. www.reuters.com/article/us-uber-spain-strike/spain-taxi-drivers-end-uber-strike-after-license-limits-agreed-idUSKBN1KN0JH.
6. https://techcrunch.com/2018/08/08/new-york-city-council-votes-to-cap-licenses-for-ride-hailing-services-like-uber-and-lyft.
7. https://en.wikipedia.org/wiki/Red_flag_traffic_laws.
8. Fredrik Erixon and Björn Weigel, The Innovation Illusion, 2016.
9. www.mynewsdesk.com/dk/arla-foods/pressreleases/en-lancering-der-gik-over-i-mejerihistorien-758271.
10. https://en.wikipedia.org/wiki/Tesla_US_dealership_disputes.
11. Fredrik Erixon and Björn Weigel, The Innovation Illusion, 2016.
12. www.dst.dk/Site/Dst/Udgivelser/nyt/GetAnalyse.aspx?cid=27867.
13. https://money.cnn.com/galleries/2009/smallbusiness/0901/gallery .founded_in_a_recession.smb/index.html.
14. https://hbr.org/2008/08/why-downturns-breed-better-innovations.
15. Richard Florida, The Great Reset: How New Ways of Living and Working Drive Post-Crash Prosperity, 2011.
16. Joseph Schumpeter, Capitalism, Socialism and Democracy, Routledge, 2010.
17. www.newandimproved.com/white-papers.aspx?NewsID=562.
18. www.oecd.org/sti/sti-outlook-2012-chapter-1-innovation-in-the-crisis-and-beyond.pdf.
19. www.oecd.org/sti/sti-outlook-2012-chapter-1-innovation-in-the-crisis-and-beyond.pdf.

PART III

INNOVATE IN THREE TRACKS

In order to make progress, one must leave the door to the unknown ajar.[1]

Richard P. Feynman

CHAPTER 9

THE EXTRA BLADE ON THE RAZOR: OPTIMIZING INNOVATION

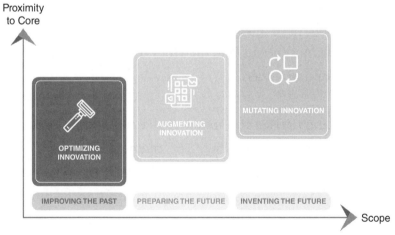

Model 3   Overview of the three innovation tracks
Source: Kris Østergaard

'To optimize' is defined in Webster's Dictionary as doing something as perfectly, effectively, or functionally as possible.[2] A successful company is a world champion in optimizing innovation. That's what most of its employees spend most of their time doing, and that's smart because that's what pays the rent and puts food on the table.

As an established organization with a certain history, optimizing innovation hasn't always been the company's focus. At one point in time, the company probably entered the market with a radically new product or a new business model that identified a gap in the market, or they succeeded because their product or business model created an unprecedented amount of value. They then built on this success, and they've worked hard to scale up and optimize through constant focus on optimization of the service, processes, and production methods. If a company is successful, this is a natural development process to undergo. They create innovations, and then they use their energy to continuously optimize them.

The challenge arises the moment that optimizations begin to create less and less value. The moment when you have metaphorically reached the razor's fifth blade and announce this year's innovation as 'now not just with four blades, but with five blades'. And the year before, you announced the year's innovation as being 'now not just with three blades, but with four blades'. You can carry out a litmus test on an organization's marketing department that shows whether or not you've reached this point. In my opinion, Robert Stephens, the founder of Geek Squad,[3] said it best. Geek Squad is a service company with 20,000 employees (founded in 1994 and acquired by Best Buy in 2002), which repairs computers and electronics for private consumers and sets itself apart by having all its employees dress as nerds and create a special experience for customers. Among other things, they wear much-too-short black pants, white socks and clip-on ties. He defined the problem very clearly and beautifully when we were gathered for the annual Think About! conference, which Pine & Gilmore, who defined the Experience Economy conceptually, have held for 20 years: 'Marketing is the price you pay for being unremarkable.' When marketing becomes the most significant thing about your product, or you start to spend excessive amounts of money performing market analyses to identify how marketing can generate new payoffs to communicate what is virtually the same product, then you're reaching the point where there are no further optimization options left for the product or service. With my background in market analysis, I can attest to the fact that (much too) many focus groups and questionnaire-based surveys have been conducted to help companies identify how they can escape their innovation issues through marketing. The answer is that marketing only works for a limited amount of time.

The more extra blades are added to the razor, the less value each new blade creates. At the same time, new companies understand when the manufacturers of various products have lost their innovation power, and they are working to make existing products redundant or to reinvent business models. This is exactly what happened to Gillette when the Dollar Shave Club almost exploded into the shaving market and gained unicorn status in a short period of time by simplifying the product, reducing the number of blades to a minimum and establishing a subscription model at an ultra-low price. Unilever bought the company when it had proven its worth, conquering 16% of the razor blade market (including 60% of the online market).[4] Procter & Gamble, which owns Gillette, had in the meantime established their own barber club, but the damage was done by then and Procter & Gamble had now got itself a huge competitor.

The world is filled with these examples. If you think about the matter of how to eat an elephant, as discussed in Chapter 5, this is exactly the zone of operation of the hundreds, if not thousands, of startups working to make one of your company's services redundant or completely transformed.

On the production and IT side, the big, established organizations are also under pressure to optimize the results, but are always lagging behind in doing so, which also impedes innovation power. Because the majority of resources go to operations, and to putting out proverbial fires. The technological debt, which every legacy organization knows only too well, accumulates year on year. They don't get the major technological upgrades or changes that they so desperately want, but make do with shortcuts and band-aids instead, because there is never enough time or money. But with that behaviour, you will find yourself in a negative spiral that you have to break out of. In the IT area, research company Gartner estimated that in 2011, $3.1 trillion (that's right, trillion with a t) was spent on IT (including hardware, services, and telecommunications). According to some of the pioneers behind the DevOps software development method,[5] it is likely that 50% of this amount was used in companies for the operation and maintenance of existing systems, and that approximately 1/3 of this half was, in turn, used for unplanned rush work – aka putting out fires. This is equivalent to $520 billion wasted on firefighting instead of on development,[6] which is clear proof of why current processes and methods do not generate enough value, and proof that there is a need for innovation methods other than optimizing innovation, even when it comes to internal organizational processes. And this is where the next innovation track comes into the picture: augmenting innovation.

The dictionary definition of augmentation is to increase, enlarge, make more intense or more complete.[7] You can compare this to augmented reality, known from, among others, Pokémon

Go. Augmented reality adds an extra layer on top of physical reality. Similarly, augmenting innovation adds an extra layer to organizations that upgrade their cores. Initially, it's a digital layer over the analogue cores of organizations, followed by necessary upgrades via, e.g. mobile technology, artificial intelligence, blockchains, and so forth in a continuous process. Doing this kind of innovation right creates a lot of new opportunities to achieve not only 2, 5, or 10% improvements but improvements by a factor of 10, thereby creating the opportunity to prepare the organization's core for the future. This requires further explanation, so let's look more deeply into how an organization can upgrade its core with augmenting innovation.

NOTES

1. Richard P. Feynman
2. www.merriam-webster.com/dictionary/optimize.
3. www.bestbuy.com/site/services/geek-squad/pcmcat138100050018.c?id=pcmcat138100050018&intl=nosplash.
4. https://medium.com/@aparacciani/seven-reasons-why-unilever-bought-dollar-shave-club-e9dc41b601fb.
5. Gene Kim et al., The DevOps Handbook: How to Create World-Class Agility, Reliability, and Security in Technology Organizations, 2016.
6. Gene Kim et al., 2016.
7. https://www.merriam-webster.com/dictionary/augment.

CHAPTER 10

IT'S NOT A SPRINT, IT'S AN ULTRAMARATHON: AUGMENTING INNOVATION

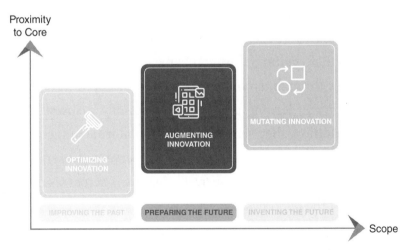

Model 3   Overview of the three innovation tracks
Source: Kris Østergaard

'We need to understand what we can use this digitization and these new business models for,' said Grundfos's management[1] to Marianne Kjeldgaard Knudsen, the current Group Vice President of the Water Utility global market segment, in Autumn 2015. It was clear to Grundfos – with its more than 70 years' proud tradition of being a global leader in supplying water pumps and solutions to all types of industries and, among other things, securing drinking water and heating for more than half a billion people worldwide – that the accelerating digitization of society would also be of great importance to them. However, how to translate this awareness into concrete initiatives was far from clear, so they decided to set up a digital taskforce to explore this particular question.

The task force, which had senior members from all parts of the organization (CEO, CFO, CIO, CMO, and Head of Innovation), formulated an 11-page document with hypotheses about the impact of digitization on the company and set out to test these hypotheses through, among other things, in-depth interviews in a network of leading people from Grundfos's closest partners. In addition, they sent their own digital frontrunners and anthropologists out into the world to observe end-users, and interviewed 72 business and private customers across six countries to test the hypotheses.

Grundfos involved both customers and collaborators in their analyses and, based on the analyses, the task force's conclusion was that it would be still a while yet before the pump itself would be challenged, and that the most meaningful thing to do would be to explore the challenges that the core business would be exposed to in the medium term in a digital world. Internet of Things solutions were, at the time of the analyses, already realizable. For example, water pumps could be connected to the outside world via sensors, so that the end user could harvest data and predict crashes before they occurred, which was of benefit to the end user as they could reduce costs by optimizing their machines' uptimes. But that was fundamentally a threat to Grundfos which, as a direct consequence of such solutions, would sell far fewer pumps in the future if the improved solutions resulted in fewer breakdowns. However, it turned out that customers had already created such innovations that Grundfos had yet to implement in their products. Customers had independently begun to develop IoT solutions for Grundfos pumps. This is often how things go, which is one of the reasons why it can be extremely valuable to conduct observation studies among customers and users, as the analyses can reveal the users' key concerns. The more challenging the users' issues are, the greater the likelihood that users have already invented solutions themselves to address the problems.

Based on the analyses, the Grundfos Task Force developed a number of digital concepts that they presented in the core company, and mobilized a group of key employees who would develop concepts further and test them with end users.

The biggest challenge that the Task Force gave itself was to make one of their traditional core products IoT-ready in just 8 weeks. However, it only took 3 days to solve the technical challenges associated with this task. The fact that a traditional production company like Grundfos – which has used waterfall-process product development methods for decades, methods which easily have a development cycle of 24–36 months – could suddenly take new technology and successfully apply it to existing products in a matter of days, instead of taking months or years, was an eye opener for the organization. In Marianne K. Knudsen's own words, it caused 'such a ruckus in the organization that they simply had to do it again and more of it'.

So how could Grundfos take this quick victory, this small successful experiment, and make sure that it didn't remain a stand-alone event, but rather ride the wave that had been created, thereby planting the seeds for a long-term strategic effort that could prepare the organization for the future by augmenting core services?

As previously described, augmenting innovation is about upgrading your core, whether it's a case of upgrading products or internal processes. Most digital transformation projects in organizations fall under the category of augmenting innovation. The first part of this journey is going from analogue to digital. As was the case with Grundfos, which had an analogue water pump and decided to digitize it. This is followed by new upgrades that will, in principle, be infinite in number, as there will always be new technological achievements that can be used to create better solutions. For example, companies become 'mobile first' because they need to be able to interact with their customers who are increasingly on the move. Or, when they move into the next augmenting phase, it's usually about implementing artificial intelligence at the core of their organization. To become 'AI first'. This is what many forward-looking companies are focusing on these days. After artificial intelligence, you could start to envision a 'quantum first' phase, if there's a breakthrough in quantum computing. For some organizations, an exploration of how certain services or processes could become 'blockchain first' would be relevant. And so on.

The answer in Grundfos on what the next step in their journey towards upgrading the core product would be was building a digital factory.

Digital Factories

Although they call it a digital factory, Grundfos's new unit is not digital, it's physical. But its task is to digitize existing products and to develop complementary digital services. Instead of setting up the unit in Berlin, Shanghai, or Silicon Valley, they decided to establish it in the very small Danish town of Bjerringbro, which is also where the headquarters are located. However, they did not physically establish the unit within the usual buildings, but in the adjacent former electronics factory. This turned out to be a stroke of genius. It gave the organization the opportunity to get the best of both worlds. They were close to the human and technological resources of the core organization which they needed to further develop core products, while residing in a completely different physical space and environment where they could act more experimentally and explore new technologies, development methods, and business models without making noise on a daily basis within the core company. In many ways, this method is similar to building a Trojan horse. It is both visible and invisible to the rest of the organization. You know it's there, but you don't quite know what's going on and not everyone has access to it. The principle of Trojan horses recurs in several of the methods that work really well for generating augmenting innovation, as we will see throughout this chapter.

As a big and established player that is launching innovation initiatives, you need to be clear on how far from or close to the core you really want to focus when kickstarting new digital projects, and on how many or few of the required resources you already possess before launching the projects.

In a case like Grundfos, the strategic decision was to upgrade the core rather than to challenge it. In other words, they would largely need to draw on existing manpower, technologies, and production methods. But it wasn't just a matter of trying to optimize what currently exists, that extra blade on the razor that we described in Chapter 9 on optimizing innovation; that was already being done very successfully within the core business. On the contrary, they wanted to experiment with creating new digital solutions and business models to expand the portfolio of services and the effect that the services could have. It required the acquisition of new digital skills, the introduction of new agile working methods, and the expectation of a higher degree of experimentation than people were used to. Therefore, it made sense to be removed from the core organization, but without losing the close relationship, as the focus was still on the core product. The majority of employees in the digital factory were recruited from within the core company, because they needed people with a deep knowledge of the core product. But at the same time, the recruited employees possessed digital skills. In fact, they were also assessed on their 'commitment', defined as their commitment to the digital agenda, which is another interesting thing. New KPIs, much like this one, were established to fit this particular new task (other KPIs that had been developed for this unit included 'entrepreneurship' and 'cooperation'); 80% of the employees' time would be spent in the digital factory to develop the new services and 20% of their time would be used in the old part of the organization to train the rest of the company on how to use the upgraded services.

Had the task been to challenge the pump, i.e. to challenge the organization's core product, and to thereby invent the future, as will be discussed in Chapter 12 on mutating innovation, then they would have needed to launch initiatives for which the existing organization didn't have any of the required resources. They would, to a much greater extent, need to find employees outside the organization with brand new capabilities, and to create new production methods using completely unprecedented technologies. If you want to come up with something new, you have to isolate yourself even more from the core company and move to the edge of the organization. But in Grundfos's case, there was a 'both/and' situation. It was about the core. But the core would also be upgraded with new technologies.

Horizontal Units

The US company GE[2] has conducted an ambitious augmentation process over the past ten years which, like the Grundfos digital factory, balances the core organization with new organizational units that are closely integrated with the core and are designated to upgrade the core and prepare GE for the future.

GE, founded as the General Electric Company by Thomas Edison in 1889, was the United States' thirteenth largest company by revenue[3] in 2017, and had over 300,000 employees.[4] GE is a conglomerate that operates in heavy industry, energy, health, and financial services. In recent years, the organization has been under financial pressure, about which things remain unclear at the time of writing this, but no matter how it ends, there are interesting lessons to learn from how GE has thoroughly digitized production and implemented what the company itself has called a digital industrial transformation. Probably the biggest digital transformation journey any traditional company has conducted in the world.

The transformation was made possible because accelerating technology development had increased performance and lowered the price of sensors so significantly that GE could now harvest data on their production facilities and customer-oriented products at unprecedented levels by integrating sensors in everything. Developments in artificial intelligence, machine learning, and deep learning had simultaneously made it possible to analyse huge data sets and extract values with a level of detail and precision that the world had not yet seen. Where the cost of digitizing production had previously been prohibitively high, GE now saw Internet of Things as 'much more than a technology trend. We began to view it as a foundational technology that could deliver material value creation and sustained competitive advantage'.[5] It also became apparent to GE that if they did not create this transformation process, they would be overtaken by new companies that were born digital and that saw a great potential to get a piece of the pie that McKinsey estimates will reach a value of 7.5 trillion dollars from 2025. According to Akanksha Manik Talya, director of GE Digital's Global Foundry Strategy and Operations, and Matt Mattox, Vice President of Industry Solutions in GE Digital, who have analysed GE's digital transformation: 'The Industrial Internet is non-optional—in the same category as electrification of industry in the last century.'[6]

So how do you digitize a company with 300,000 employees? You do it one step at a time, but with an extremely high level of ambition. In the first part of this book, I addressed the fact that it is necessary to sharpen the axe before commencing work. GE did the same. Thorough analyses were carried out of the capabilities, tools, and processes that they already possessed and used at factories, along with analyses of the gap between existing and required capabilities. Through these, it was decided that the capabilities and tools needed to develop in the process should be horizontally available. That is to say, there was a conscious effort to ensure that factories across the organization were all able to benefit from the process, rather than risking various business units' isolation due to the traditional silos that GE knew only too well. In addition, GE Digital was established, a new independent business unit that was to operate across the other existing business units. You could call it another type of Trojan horse. Each business unit was established with a Chief Digital Officer function, who reported both to their own business unit and to the overall digital management team, in order to optimize the potential for synergies.

The next step was to connect existing infrastructure, software stacks and processes to collect and process future data, and to ensure integration between business units and departments within individual business units so that the backend and frontend could work together. This required the hiring of a number of new employees with software and computer skills that the organization hadn't previously possessed. But process optimization was not just about connecting and optimizing internal processes. On the contrary, they expanded their partner-ecosystem with an open innovation mindset and established partner programmes, so that they could innovate with distributors, technology partners, and developers. That decision also optimized GE's potentials for success, because 49% of the most important product innovations in manufacturing companies actually originate from input from external sources, according to an analysis discussed by the Professor for Strategy at Washington University, Anne Marie Knott, in her book *How Innovation Really Works*.[7]

Before initiating innovation at the business model level as the final step of the process, i.e. moving from making internally directed process optimizations to engaging in externally targeted product optimizations and developments, a cultural journey was initiated that entailed the introduction of a new set of values called 'GE Beliefs', which focused on optimizing customer centricity, faster development and learning processes, and included a special focus on getting each employee involved in strengthening and inspiring their colleagues. This work was anchored in a method that GE calls FastWorks, and that is best described as the lean startup method. This makes sense as the process was developed with Eric Ries, the man who made that term popular in his book *The Lean Startup*.[8] The lean startup method uses a three-part continuous cycle, in which you build simple versions of products (MVPs – minimum viable products), expose customers or users to the product, collect data on their experiences, and improve the product based on these inputs in close collaboration with other suppliers until you have a product you can vouch for. In order to cement this change, 3000 leaders were trained in the methods to ensure internalization of the methodologies and the new values across the organization.[9]

A practical example of results created with the FastWorks method, which can be described as a classic augmenting case in relation to production, is the upgrade of GE's kitchen and white goods division based on the principles we have just discussed. Their first self-assigned product development task was to develop a refrigerator with French doors, i.e. with double glass doors. The work process was to be carried out with an unprecedentedly small team, without much money, and within only three months, and the refrigerator was to be on the market within a year.[10] A not insignificant challenge in a culture that traditionally launches new products in 5-year cycles. Many said that the problem was impossible to solve. However, through the lean startup principles, it actually succeeded.

To break it down, GE has done the following:

1) Analysed the organization's need to prepare for the future.
2) Developed processes and tools needed in the long term, in a form where an independent digital unit has been established that also works cross-functionally to ensure synergy and horizontal integration.
3) Worked with upgrading capabilities and creating a new culture, where the employees have the right tools and thrive in the new reality.

You might be thinking 'Gosh – it's a massive effort, it has taken years to launch, and it has cost huge amounts of money.' And you would be right. You might also be thinking, 'We are not GE, so how could we possibly do the same thing?' To that I would say: think of best principles rather than best practice. Best practice is where you look at those who are similar to yourself, and then copy what they are doing well. With best principles, on the other hand, you are looking at those who are different from yourself, not to copy what they do, but to identify what they are doing, in order to then translate the principles of that into your own universe. You shouldn't faithfully copy GE's approach. You shouldn't, for that matter, want to faithfully copy Grundfos or any other company. You should observe the principles of what the other companies are doing, then – through your own analyses, as you are sharpening the axe – investigate what you need to learn and how to translate what you've learned into your own unique universe.

Rome was not built in a day, and a good place to start could be by establishing a centre of excellence where you have the opportunity to practice and to make the application of these methods come naturally to you. It is a method that has spread further and further across established organizations in recent years, for when they want to use and spread new technology internally.

CENTRES OF EXCELLENCE

What should you do if you can see that automations are the way forward? When you are convinced that you will have to upgrade the organization to be carried by artificial intelligence and you decide, on a more basic level, that chatbots, for instance, are the first step to bringing your customer service into the twenty-first century?

First and foremost, you need the right technological capabilities. Maybe you possess them internally, but it is more likely that you will need to find at least some of them externally. The person(s) to be employed to drive this development must be highly skilled because they have to build capabilities and products from scratch and teach the organization how to do things. There aren't many people who possess both the technological and the entrepreneurial skills required to establish new units in technological niche fields. Therefore, it is difficult to recruit the right forces and, therefore, you have to make sure that you make them a particularly attractive offer. That is one of the core values of creating a centre of excellence – the opportunity to design a unit that is an occupational land of milk and honey for the right people, who will then have the opportunity to play their way forward to the best solutions in a unit that is exclusively dedicated to the one task.

According to Andrew Ng, who has run the artificial intelligence rollout in both the Chinese giant Baidu and in Amazon, the opportunity to attract the right capabilities is one of the main reasons for building a centre of excellence. That was Baidu's experience, when they switched to mobile platforms in 2011 and, initially, couldn't attract the best skill sets. This was also their experience when they were about to build their first artificial intelligence units.[11] Nonetheless, the units were built within the organization, because it was important that they were close by, as the assignment was to prepare the company for the future by upgrading the core. Again, the principle was to build a Trojan horse, as discussed in relation to the digital factories. You remain very close to the core, but you also wall off the unit from the outside world so that it can experiment in peace.

When building a large-scale centre of excellence – like in Baidu's case where the innovation process is about becoming 'AI first', i.e. ensuring the integration of artificial intelligence into the company's processes and products – you have to think and work differently than you would in a traditional Internet company. Ng describes, among other things, how Baidu had to go from being an Internet company, where data reside in individual organizational silos, to becoming an artificial intelligence company in which integrated data warehouses are built outside the silos. There has also been a shift from employing project managers who are masters of sketching wireframes, to hiring and educating artificial intelligence engineers who can't use those kinds of sketches for anything. Instead, they base their work on a discussion of the kinds of conversations a chatbot should be able to conduct, in order to train project managers on how to produce data sets that engineers can then convert into actions. So it's a matter of fundamentally new ways to approach development tasks, which requires new teams with new capabilities that are also able to recruit further employees when the need to expand the team arises.

After building the appropriate unit and developing its services, the next step is organizational integration enabling the rest of the organization to learn from its centre of excellence. Therefore, a centre of excellence should also act as a training unit for the organization through cross-organizational projects. That is, key employees from other parts of the organization are invited to the company's centre of excellence and trained in its methods, or they collaborate to integrate the new technologies, processes, or products into other parts of the organization.

In Amazon, for instance, there were a lot of artificial intelligence projects distributed across many different departments, but there was no knowledge sharing and no synergies across the organization. By creating a central unit responsible for machine learning projects that launched interorganizational projects, this integration was achieved. They amplified the exchanges to cover the entire company and upgraded the core organization in its goal of becoming 'AI first'.[12] TDC, the Danish telecom company, initially built a centre of excellence revolving about the development of chatbots. After building their first chatbot, they invited core employees from the rest of the organization to educate them in the skills that they had developed, so that they could be spread further across the organization.

Centres of excellence help upgrade the core, train the organization in how to work with new technology, develop new services, and harvest faster and better gains than traditional silo-based development. A unit is established within the core with the purpose of upgrading the organization. You develop the skills and services you need and, when the right moment comes, you move on to spread these skills to the rest of the organization.

Internal and external accelerators serve as other methods for increasing the organizational innovation capacity to upgrade the core, either through collaborating with startups whose core services are closely linked to the core organization's needs, or through creating your own startup teams.

EXTERNAL ACCELERATORS

Plug and Play is an accelerator factory in the heart of Silicon Valley, which had an unlikely beginning as office space lessor at 165 University Avenue in Palo Alto. A building also known as The Lucky Building – a fairly regular two-story property with an unusual history that has given it its name. In the 1990s, Saeed Amidi, the owner of the building who was also a real estate investor and carpet dealer, was renting out a space in the property to a new startup company called Google, which didn't have much money. Therefore, Amidi agreed to take a small share in the company in order to keep rent low. A business model that he also used when another small startup named PayPal also needed an office and was similarly tight on money.

Not too many years passed before those investments proved to be astronomically lucrative.

The early success that Amidi experienced from taking shares in startups gave him such a taste for it that he decided to extend his efforts to activities besides renting out office space, and to actively help entrepreneurs scale. It was the start of Plug and Play, which currently operates more than 50 accelerator programmes worldwide with hundreds of startups from almost every industry imaginable (retail, insurance, blockchain, Internet of Things, logistics, food, energy, etc.).

As discussed in the first part of the book, it is imperative that a big well-established player knows which startups are the most attractive in order to identify both potential competitors and collaborators. Plug and Play's accelerators are a simple and relatively cost-effective way to find collaborators that can help upgrade the company's core. Every year, they screen thousands of startups that apply to join the accelerator programmes. Only a few, around 20 per programme, pass through the eye of the needle. The established companies that sponsor the accelerator programmes weigh in on which startups are selected, and from there they have the opportunity to track the development of the startup companies, and to begin collaborating with them. Hence, they don't have to build products, technological capabilities, or business models from the ground up internally

TRANSFORMING LEGACY ORGANIZATIONS

in their own organizations, as these entrepreneurs have already spent years doing it.

In my company, we brought a management group from a leading pharmaceutical company with us to Silicon Valley. Among other things, we visited Plug and Play to meet interesting startups. One of these startups was working on a problem – that two of the leading employees from our client's research and development department told us – that the internal part of their organization had, for several years, considered developing and investing a substantial million-dollar amount into. The leaders of the pharmaceutical company had no idea that there were already entrepreneurs around the world who were working on the same problem and were years ahead of their own research and development. By engaging directly with a startup that has already done the preliminary work and made a lot of mistakes, a traditional company can skip a lot of development steps and save a lot of money. A startup would be interested in collaborating with big companies because they can gain access to all the resources that they don't have, but which the established companies have in abundance, e.g. customers, infrastructure, and data. It's a pure win-win situation.

Today, there is a large number of external accelerators around the world that allow established companies to find, and collaborate with, the most interesting startups. Techstars, 500 Startups,

Startupbootcamp, and Plug and Play are some of the most successful. The vast majority of accelerators have been made to be of value to the established companies by helping them upgrade the core. That is to say, the intention is to find startups that already have either proof of concept or proof of product (i.e. they have proven that the concept or product is sustainable to a certain degree), and to build bridges between them and the companies that have a concrete need of upgrading their core deliverables.

However, there are also accelerators like Singularity University's Global Startup programme, that focus more on helping established companies challenge the core and engage in mutating innovation, i.e. far more long-term initiatives. In this accelerator programme, well-established companies can sponsor startups that undergo a one-year development process with the aim of creating solutions that can take the companies in new directions. Other accelerators such as Y Combinator – which, so far, has been the most successful of all – have been more focused on helping startups find funding from venture capitalists, scale to unicorn status, and, to a lesser extent, initiate partnerships between startups and established companies. When you, as an established company, carry out your analyses of the existing collaboration opportunities with accelerator programmes, you therefore need to focus closely on the perspective of the programmes, as this can be crucial to the potential value they can create.

INTERNAL ACCELERATORS

More and more companies of a certain size are beginning to see the value of creating their own accelerator programmes. The benefits here, in contrast to those of cooperating with external accelerators, are that you have more ownership, more control of the process and increased proximity to the projects that are developed as it's all happening in your own backyard. This could potentially be a big advantage, as one of the biggest challenges established companies face when working with external accelerators is the issue of creating sustainable collaborations between the core company and the external startups. This may be due to challenges such as: sharing IP rights for the services developed; where to anchor the partnership within the core organization; not speaking the same language or understanding each other's work cultures; or lacking processes for the integration of the new services or technologies that the startup company contributes. All are barriers to a successful exchange if you don't handle the challenges properly. If you create your own internal accelerator, you can avoid these barriers. However, you need to be aware that it is more resource-intensive to create your own accelerator. An internal accelerator programme can cost millions, while, in some cases, you can engage with external accelerators for just a few hundred thousand dollars. It also requires you to possess the key skills for, and experience of, developing and implementing such programmes in order to tailor the training that startups need, to make sure that they feel that they fit into the environment, that they are given the mentoring they need, that they are put in touch with the right partners in the development process, and so on.

At CA Technologies, an American software company that has been recognized by Forbes as one of the world's 100 most innovative companies,[13] an internal accelerator has been established and organizationally anchored under the CTO. According to their then Vice President of Strategy, George Watt, as he shared at the innovation festival South by South West, the purpose of the accelerator is threefold: partly developing services that can contribute to the core organization's portfolio, partly strengthening the organization's innovation culture by upgrading its competencies, and partly being included in the company's branding, enabling the company to attract new employees by creating what is called corporate entrepreneurship – entrepreneurship within the company – which has become an attraction parameter in the fight for talents.

The establishment of this internal accelerator has been another step in a maturation process for CA Technologies, where the first step was to collaborate with an external accelerator to gain experience. Creating your own accelerator programme is no small task. Money is only a small part of the problem. The most important thing is that you have the capabilities and experiences to develop a successful accelerator. By collaborating with an external accelerator and learning from this experience, you can harvest important experiences and use them as part of a kind of lean startup process, where the collaboration acts as a prototype, after which you can evaluate and measure the results in order to learn and develop further so that you can create your own programme.

When evaluating a startup's attractiveness as an investment in the early stages, any reasonable investor will say that the team is the most important parameter. This is because the only thing you can use to assess potential in the beginning is the small group of people wanting to act on an idea. Experience precisely shows that the foundation for successful startups is the execution drive to a far greater extent than it is the idea itself. There are plenty of ideas, and there are always several people trying to realize the same ideas. But there are precious few people who have the abilities and the energy to realize the ideas, and the persistence that it takes to overcome all the obstacles on the journey towards creating a sustainable business based on these ideas. The people you select to run the projects are, therefore, the alpha and omega. Having the right candidates run an internal entrepreneurial project, like an accelerator, is as important as having the right founders of a startup. When the internal accelerator at CA Technologies was first established, candidates were found internally through marketing and competitions. In the selection process, candidates were not only asked to pitch their ideas, but also to pitch themselves so that management could understand their motivations for participating in the process, and so that they could gain an impression of the applicants' strengths and weaknesses. It was also interesting to note that founders of startups previously purchased by the company, who were still employed by the company, were extremely good candidates for the accelerator. Giving them the opportunity to run entrepreneurial projects internally in the company was both a way of utilizing their particular entrepreneurial skills and maintaining their commitment to the company.

A tightly controlled acceleration process was also established, and an infrastructure was built, to handle this process in order to acid test and support the concepts on their journey from idea to sustainable business. An investment board was set up that decided which ideas would pass through the eye of the needle. There is always a senior management member in this board to ensure commitment from the top. The teams that develop the ideas start small, just like a real startup, and only expand their teams when the ideas prove to be sustainable. In exchange, they have a support network in the organization in the form of access to internal experts, such as the research and development or sales department, where they can both gain inspiration and access technology, data, or customers. Only the fewest of startups have such an advantage out in 'the real world'.

If the projects survive, the investment board ends up deciding how the projects will end. In the normal world of entrepreneurship, the end comes when the founders sell their company. But in internal accelerators, the end could be the integration of a technology into the core company, if that has been the focus of the project; producing a service; or even considering whether to establish a new company to scale up and sell the product. Another interesting self-evaluation measurement point that CA Technologies created to use the internal accelerator to strengthen the entire organization's innovation culture is the accelerator's ability to, for example, transfer the agile work methods used in accelerator projects back into the core organization. This also makes the internal accelerator an important tool in developing the entire company's culture.

Ericsson, one of the world's leading communications companies – with 140 years of existence to its name[14] – does something similar. If you visit their Silicon Valley design centre, you can not only take a tour of their state-of-the-art experience centre, you can also meet the people who run their newly established and highly ambitious internal accelerator. The goal is to create internal entrepreneurial projects that turn into at least one unicorn per year, i.e. has a business potential of at least one billion dollars. As with CA Technologies, the method is that of implementing a tightly controlled development process. In the first four weeks, ideas are developed. Then the people who developed the ideas are invited to present them to a panel, like the ones we've seen in shows like *Shark Tank*. The ideas that the panel considers to be strong enough move on to a four-month incubation process, where analyses and prototypes are produced, then tested and matured into concrete concepts. The next acid test is a meeting with an investment panel that decides whether the concepts should move on to the final phase, a scaling process that can extend for over 24 months. A key criterion is that the concepts have the potential to reach a value of $500 million over three years.

According to Goetz Kursawe, the head of Ericsson's Silicon Valley Innovation Center, 92 ideas were pitched in the first year of running the accelerator. From these, 10–15 projects were moved on to the incubation process. Hence, most were eliminated. It is still too early to say how successful these projects will become, but a crucial point, which is often forgotten, is that you need many ideas to generate one winner. I often meet companies that think that innovation is about heavily investing in one idea. And I meet just as many companies that don't implement a strict idea development process to find this one idea, but instead focus on ideas that have been in the drawer and have been discussed for a number of years, or those which randomly appear and are therefore primarily valued because they are top of mind with management. However, these are dangerous methods that optimize the risk of failure. Idea development and maturation should be a rigorous process that is taken as seriously as legacy organizations typically take their traditional product development processes.

Internal accelerators offer the best of both worlds when it comes to augmenting innovation that upgrades the core: you create an optimized process for developing new innovations, thus upgrading the company's capabilities and innovation culture. But you do it in a much safer way, partly because internal accelerator project owners don't risk everything by engaging in the project the way startup founders do, and partly because there are many lifelines connected to the parent organization that can provide support through access to customers, data, technology, and money.

There is an inherent risk that projects will fail or won't release their full potential if the employees who set up the internal entrepreneurship projects don't invest enough of themselves into the projects. It's what you call having 'skin in the game'. It's easier to give up when things get really difficult – which, when you create something from scratch, it always does at some point – than it is, by nature, for an entrepreneur who doesn't have a big organization backing them up. They can always go back to their old job if nothing comes of the projects. In my opinion, this is one of the dangers of using lean startup rhetoric, where failing is a positive word. I understand the intention behind the use of this rhetorical device. Many analyses show that major organizations' 'no-mistakes-allowed' culture impedes innovation and development, and it's also true that idea development, maturation and scaling are lengthy processes, in which you constantly acid test with the aim of killing, which is a good thing. But we see examples of the rhetorical focus on failure, which is adopted by certain established organizations when they develop more entrepreneurial processes, become easy arguments for giving up. That's why I like to talk about, and celebrate, persistence. Persistence comes after the mistakes. If you are persistent, you don't give up when things get tough.

However, the greatest risk for not getting optimal value from internal accelerators usually comes from senior management in one of two ways. The first is when management loses its commitment. There are many examples of how it's easier to get permission and a budget to kickstart innovation projects than it is to renew the budgets or extend the projects once the honeymoon phase is over and you're left with results that aren't as speedy or big as you had hoped. The second way in which this risk manifests itself is when management doesn't take the initiatives seriously enough. A senior manager from a major IT organization we worked with told us how an internal accelerator project he had launched was discussed by other members of the management like it was play-pretend. Management didn't appreciate how much commitment and how much pride and ambition the intrapreneurs had for the projects, or the amount of potential that could be released from actual success. Expectations were low, despite the fact that management had allocated millions to the project. Low expectations can easily turn into self-fulfilling prophecies. Senior management's lack of ambition and appreciation of their employees' ambitions becomes the biggest risk factor for the creation of innovation theatre instead of innovation culture.

It's Not a Sprint, It's an Ultramarathon

I meet many top executives who talk about digital transformation, or other change and innovation initiatives that can be categorized as augmenting innovation, like they are projects that will ultimately end. 'Gee, this automation process is tough. Can't wait till it's over.' And of course, projects will end. But augmenting innovation is fundamentally a process that never stops. Because the first phase of a digital transformation process is when you digitize the analogue. If you are an established organization with many years behind you, you will have a lot of analogue systems and IT that cause problems in a world of increasing competition and the need for individualization of products and services. Therefore, you need to digitize the analogue and reap the new fruits that digitization creates. But development doesn't stop there. The need for augmenting innovation remains. Take Google, for instance, one of the most prominent names in this context. They are thoroughly digitized. They are 'mobile first'. They have understood how to adapt their core products – searches and advertising – to a world where users mainly search on their mobile devices. Facebook has been through a similar development. However, the leading digital companies are now talking about the next wave of augmentation: becoming 'AI first'. Because the companies mentioned have not yet been augmented with artificial intelligence. That is the next part of the development. If you've observed Google's activities just over the past year, you can see that they take this task very seriously. Google has established two artificial intelligence-focused investment funds, purchased three artificial intelligence companies, become the leader in obtaining patents for speech recognition, and optimized their focus on neural networks in their latest patent applications.[15] Likewise with Amazon. They hire AI experts far quicker than everyone else, and have job listings for more than 41% of all the AI jobs that are applied for across the United States.[16]

After 'AI first', a new augmentation need will arise. Perhaps it will be becoming 'quantum first' and using the enormous potentials of quantum computing. And so on, and so forth. You probably know the expression 'It's not a sprint, it's a marathon', which is often used when leaders talk about the need to act persistently and with the long term in mind. My assertion is that augmenting innovation, and innovation overall, should not be thought of as a marathon, but as an ultramarathon. Because every day you cross the finish line, you know that tomorrow brings a new finish line. You need to get comfortable with this, and that means understanding how to transform your culture, the next crucial effort we will be looking into.

NOTES

1. www.grundfos.com.
2. www.ge.com.
3. https://en.wikipedia.org/wiki/General_Electric.
4. www.statista.com/statistics/220718/number-of-employees-at-general-electric.
5. GE's Digital Industrial Transformation Playbook, 2016.
6. GE's Digital Industrial Transformation Playbook, 2016.
7. Anne Marie Knott, How Innovation Really Works: Using the Trillion-Dollar R&D Fix to Drive Growth, 2017.
8. Eric Ries, The Lean Startup, 2011.
9. https://gereports.ca/fastworks.
10. https://hbr.org/2014/04/how-ge-applies-lean-startup-practices.
11. www.youtube.com/watch?v=NKpuX_yzdYs.
12. www.wired.com/story/amazon-artificial-intelligence-flywheel.
13. www.ca.com/us/company/company-information.html.
14. www.ericsson.com/en.
15. CB Insights: Google Strategy Teardown, 2018.
16. http://careerbright.com/hiring/new-paysa-study-reveals-u-s-companies-across-all-industries-investing-1-35-billion-dollars-in-ai-talent.

CHAPTER 11

FROM STATUS QUO TO CONTINUOUS INNOVATION: CULTURE HACKS

It is vital that an organization has a strong innovation culture if augmenting innovation is to take place within its core. And that culture is unfortunately not present in all companies. Many established organizations have a status quo culture, as we discussed in Chapter 2, when we reviewed the status quo bias – the one that causes you to prefer avoiding loss over winning. This attitude is a barrier to change and holds innovation back. Therefore, many established organizations will need to transform the culture of their organization from being a status quo culture into a culture where all employees are incremental innovators.

Here, I define an incremental innovator as someone who thrives in constant change, within certain boundaries. It is important to emphasize that we are talking about change within certain boundaries, because those within the mother organization are working to upgrade the core, not to challenge the core. When challenging the core, you need radical innovators who thrive in constant change without boundaries. But you don't want too many of them in the core organization, because this would lead to chaos and anarchy.

Radical innovators are a special type of people who have a high tolerance for risk. They are overrepresented among startup founders and people who practise extreme sports. They are the ones who think it's cool to draw their pension and put all the money into a project that is unlikely to succeed. They're the ones who climb mountains with their bare hands, without climbing ropes, and have a great time doing it. There are few truly radical innovators in the world. There are even fewer of them in large, established companies, and those who are there can be hard to find, but are extremely valuable. The radical innovators you may have hired could be there without you knowing. They may be invisible, poor performers, or the types of people you find annoying and strange. They may be the people you want to fire the most. And that might also be the right thing to do. However, you first need to consider whether they may be poor performers and annoying because they, as radical innovators, are in the wrong job. Just like Einstein, who, legend has it, was terrible in school and didn't speak before he was six years old, but nevertheless was the one to uncover the relativity theories. You probably have valuable unidentified capabilities in the organization in the form of radical innovators who, if they had the right framework to work within, could achieve not only true job satisfaction, but real success for the organization when it comes to mutating innovation – the theme of the next chapter.

For the incremental innovator, the profile we want to see predominating at our organizations' cores, the optimal zone for innovation is in the sweet spot where the risks and consequences of failing are neither too big nor too small. If the consequences are too small, you're not putting anything on the line and you get bored. If the consequences are too big, you get scared and have a harder time generating results. Therefore, it is important to find the right balance and to ensure that the changes that are being made happen within these limits.

In fact, everyone possesses the ability to be good innovators. We are all born like this. But most of us unlearn these abilities through spending much of our lives within the tightly controlled systems that are constituted by our educational institutions and workplaces. A large 10-year study of 1,600 children which tested their creativity – defined as the ability to engage in divergent thinking, i.e. the ability to have original ideas which differ from anything you have ever seen before – measured the creativity of children who were 5, 10, and 15 years old. Then the results were compared to those of 280,000 adults. As five-year-olds, 98% of the children were considered to be creative geniuses, but over time, their natural creativity levels fell. Among 10-year-olds, the percentage had already fallen to 32%, among 15-year-olds they were down to 10%, and among adults only 2% were creative geniuses. If those numbers don't give you pause, I don't know what will.[1]

These results also explain why our organizations lack innovation power. As citizens, we unlearn our skills of divergent thinking, and most of our organizations are built to promote and maintain this state. The organizations may have been founded by people who were creative geniuses, but unless the founders still run the organizations and are very visible bearers of the culture, the organizations quickly change and are left to people who have largely unlearned divergent thinking, and have rather learned convergent thinking, which is the ability to be critical. Criticism is also important. The problem is that we spend too much time in our organizations being critical and not enough time being creative. There's simply a lack of balance.

The good news is that if you can unlearn your creativity, you can also relearn it. You can do this by implementing a series of cultural hacks, where you consciously develop your innovation culture. By cultural hacks, I mean initiatives that directly influence the company's culture and are strong enough to lead to cultural change. Model 4 shows the design elements you need to focus on to strengthen your innovation culture. It revolves around the company's scenes, agents, and processes. The model was initially introduced to me by my co-founder at SingularityU Nordic, Laila Pawlak, and we further developed it in our work on understanding and designing optimal customer experiences. However, the model is equally valuable when it comes to developing organizational culture. And the amazing thing is that the vast majority of implementable cultural hacks are free.

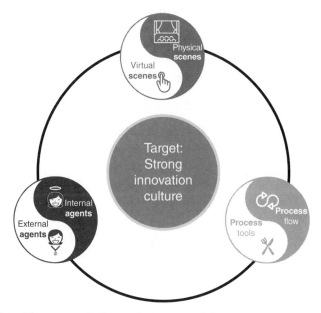

Model 4   Elements to Enhance Innovation Culture
Source: Laila Pawlak & Kris Østergaard

SCENES, AGENTS, AND PROCESSES

There are four basic elements in the model. The central core we will here define as a culture in which incremental innovators truly thrive. To optimize the likelihood of actually creating this culture, you can use the three other basic elements as support tools. Just like you can adjust the bass, treble, and balance on a stereo (if anyone can remember what a stereo is) for a better sonic experience, you can adjust scenes, processes, and agents to create a better innovation culture.

The first support tool comprises the scenes. That's everything you can see, hear, smell, feel, and taste. In modern times, you have to categorize scenes into both digital and physical scenes, as we are increasingly living our lives digitally. But scenes are basically our material experiences. Office interiors play a surprisingly significant role: lighting, sounds, scents, and decor. All of it affects us as human beings; largely on an unconscious level, but with great importance to our productivity, innovation power, and job satisfaction.

The second support tool, the agents, are ourselves, and the agents we interact with. Originally, Laila Pawlak and I called this model element 'people', but in line with the robotization of our society, it now makes sense to say 'agents'. Agents can also be divided into two parts, internal and external agents. In a cinema, the internal agents are the employees who are working to help customers buy tickets and popcorn. But they are, increasingly, also the machines where you pick up and print your tickets. The external agents are the other cinema-goers. They also affect the overall experience of going to the cinema. We all know what it feels like to sit in the cinema and be absorbed by a movie, to then be disturbed by someone two rows ahead whose phone rings. It ruins the movie experience. Basically, it's not the cinema's fault that this happens. But the cinema knows that ringing phones destroy the overall movie experience, so the cinema takes responsibility and shows some fun informational videos that remind the cinema-goers that they need to turn off their mobile phones.

The third support tool consists of processes – that is, the ways we do things. The flows we go through from point A to point B to point C, and the tools we use. Let me exemplify using a trip to the supermarket, a situation we're all very familiar with. In the supermarket, one flow is, for instance, that milk is always at the back of the store. It's there, because everyone needs milk. (This is actually not completely true, as milk sales are in crisis. But let's say skyr instead. Now everyone needs skyr.) Supermarkets are extremely aware of this fact, so they send customers all the way to the back of the store because that flow increases sales, as people make more impulse purchases on their way to the milk (or the skyr). Supermarket tools include, for instance, carts and baskets. When the supermarkets began adding wheels on the baskets, they increased sales because people no longer had to carry their shopping. As the supermarkets increased cart sizes, people also began to buy more because it took longer to fill up the cart and to get a sense of how much had been bought. For the same reason, some canteens and buffet restaurants have introduced small plates so that they fill up quicker. It creates the perception that you have more food on the plate and, hence, people eat less, and the restaurants save money on food purchases and reduce food waste.

The physical and virtual scenes, internal and external agents, and process flows and tools are as important to customer experiences as they are to employee experiences. You can therefore use the design elements of the model to develop your innovation culture and build a variety of cultural hacks into each element, creating a culture that is designed to promote and support innovation at the core of the organization.

Scenes That Strengthen Innovation Culture

'My biggest innovation challenge right now is booking a meeting room for a full day so my team can meet up.' A participant told me this during a break on one of our educational programmes after we had discussed how to create a strong innovation culture.

His interjection says something about the challenges that many executives and employees face in their daily work. Sometimes, the most banal things serve as obstacles to people's opportunities for creating better results. A lack of meeting rooms is a problem in virtually all companies. You have to book rooms far in advance, which is a barrier to, for example, quickly gathering when new ideas arise. Often, you can only book rooms for short periods of time, which makes it impossible to have the time to dive deep into a problem. The problem of rooms is often difficult to solve, because square meters are a costly expense in short supply, and once you have set up interiors in a particular way, it becomes expensive and difficult to change. As always, it pays to do things right from the beginning, but there are a lot of cultural hacks you can consider implementing to turn your scenes from obstacles into allies.

First and foremost, the open office environments that have been the preferred design principle for many years are a very bad idea if you want employees to be able to concentrate. You simply cannot concentrate in an environment where you are constantly exposed to interference, constantly seeing other people out of the corner of your eye, and always involuntarily taking part in other people's conversations. Some studies indicate that it takes up to 15 minutes to regain optimal concentration levels after having been disturbed.[2] In an open office environment, there will never be more than 15 minutes between interruptions, which means that people working in open office environments never get the chance to enter an optimal state of concentration. A study conducted by the psychologists Banbury and Berry – from Cardiff and Reading universities, respectively – shows that you can improve performance by 16% if you let people work in a quiet environment rather than in open office environments, and it can even improve by 40% in cases where people are working on difficult calculation assignments.[3] Overall, the constant interruptions that many face every day at the office mean that they lose an average of up to 70 minutes of productivity over an eight-hour workday.[4] If you want to give your employees the optimal conditions to create value, one place to start is the open office.

Open environments are fine when you don't have to do work that requires concentration, but you want to be inspired. Just like most of us enjoy sitting in a cafe on a busy street and having a cup of coffee while people-watching and absorbing the atmosphere, you can design areas in your office environment for the same purpose. Open areas where people can meet and be inspired. Such places can create renewed energy during breaks throughout the day, so that you can subsequently continue your concentration work. The open areas can also be of value by facilitating meetings between people who may not otherwise see each other during a working day.

The IT company Sun Microsystems, which was acquired by Oracle in 2009, conducted an analysis that showed that variety in office interiors also has an impact on productivity. By ensuring that employees were able to choose between office environments with varied interiors that lend themselves to meet-ups and informal conversations, and to concentration work, they experienced 10% increased individual productivity and 7% increased team productivity.[5]

We can also identify significant impacts on productivity by examining details such as room temperature, lighting and differences in artificial and natural light. If employees are able to adjust the room temperature themselves, this can increase productivity by 3.5%; the right lighting can increase productivity by 6.7%; and if you additionally ensure access to natural lighting and a window with a view, this can increase productivity by between 9–12%, according to the *Journal of Facility Management Education and Research*.[6]

As humans, we get attached to our physical surroundings. For example, psychologists have shown that being asked to change offices can affect us greatly and cause a sense of loss. If, on the other hand, we have an influence on our office environment design, this also strengthens our psychological well-being and job satisfaction.[7] At Maersk Growth, the logistics and shipping giant's venture unit – which we will revisit in the next chapter on mutating innovation – employees have their own offices away from the core organization, and they have independently designed the entire office to create a personal environment which everyone thrives in, without any involvement of interior designers. The method has the added benefit that it is super-cheap. Grundfos's digital factory even changes its layout on a regular basis, so that employees continuously experience change. Neurology research shows that change, under the right circumstances, creates enthusiasm. According to neuroscientist David Eagleman, people have a reaction pattern called repetition suppression, which means that every time the brain is exposed to the same stimuli, it reacts less to them. It adapts to its surroundings. The disadvantage of this is that the less surprising our environment is, the less energy we use to relate to things around us. Shaking things up every now and again stirs up the mind and our curiosity, and we get that bit more excited. This is good for innovation.[8]

In my company, we have a 70,000 square foot campus that serves as a co-working space for entrepreneurs, as innovation offices for established companies, and as event venues which we rent out and use for our own training programmes. Here, we have tried to integrate the above research to create an environment that is as motivating and productive as possible. The companies design their own offices so that they can put their personal touch on them, but we are responsible for the common areas, and we design them to suit private conversations, informal meetings in an open environment where high levels of concentration aren't required, and mingling on every floor at kitchenettes and coffee stops. Everyone eats lunch in the canteen, which we call the Moonshot Cafe. The environment is decorated with many colours and art on the walls, with themes relating (tongue-in-cheek) to our company's purpose, i.e. technological development, the interaction between people and technology, and positive impact. This includes a lamp made out of an old hair dryer, a chair made of computer keyboards, or a version of Michelangelo's Sistine Chapel with robots instead of humans. All common area spots have reading material which includes many different books on the most important topics of the time, as well as magazines such as *MIT Management Review, Nature, New Scientist, Time, Fortune, Inc Magazine, Harvard Business Review,* etc., so that you can always be inspired by the latest stories or research. Finally, there are living plants in as many places as possible. The goal is not only to make the campus area nice to be in, but also to stimulate people's intelligence and surprise them with design details to constantly exercise their curiosity and openness.

Of course, the physical environment is complemented by digital tools that determine the functionality of the physical spaces and to support modern forms of collaboration. For example, on every floor, we have beams, monitors that stand 1.5 m tall and can be remotely controlled via the computer keyboard – a kind of mobile Skype. With them, you can attend not only meetings without being physically present; you can actually move about the office if you need to. We have a Slack channel for all employees and residents. Slack is a messenger service that enables quick, collective, and personal messages that are easier to use than emails when it comes to sending short messages. There are, of course, also digital solutions which enable clear and easy bookings of office rooms and lunch.

In summary: even in our digital age, you can't underestimate the importance of the physical working environment to support productivity, well-being, and innovation. Our physical spaces may become even more important precisely because we spend so much time in digital spaces on a daily basis, even though opportunities to combine physical and digital spaces are also necessary. By using the aforementioned principles that have proven effects, you can use your scenes to create culture hacks that help the organization develop a stronger innovation culture.

Agents That Strengthen Innovation Culture

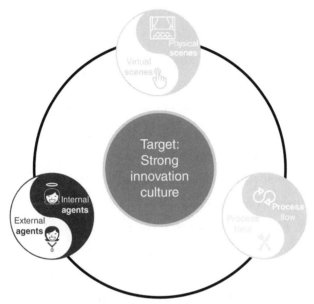

Model 4   Elements to Enhance Innovation Culture

Agents are the people – or machines – that we interact with, and this, of course, includes ourselves. When working on creating a culture where everyone has the opportunity to become incremental innovators within the core of the organization, it is, of course, extremely important to focus on this element. In order to create such a strong innovation culture, everyone must relearn creativity. In this context it is important to create a psychologically safe space for people so that they feel safe enough to embark on projects with unknown results. Finally, it is important that you, as a company, address the controversial subject of diversity.

The good news is that we as human beings can actually rediscover our creativity. The two brain researchers Morten Friis-Olivarius and Balder Onarheim have researched this through a process that, within eight weeks, raised the test subjects' divergent thinking ability by 28.5%.[9] The researchers – as researchers tend to – used their students as test subjects, and introduced neuroscience insights on the mechanics of human creativity into their teaching. Then they uncovered the students' ability to thinking divergently using pre- and post-tests (i.e. questionnaire surveys where the same questions were asked before and after the experiment to compare changes), and compared the results with a control group that did not undergo the same process.

Overall, the students underwent a process where they first learned to understand the neuroscientific explanations of creativity, that is, the reasons why the brain acts the way it does in connection with creativity. Next, they learned about the differences between divergent thinking (getting new ideas) and convergent tools (criticizing/qualifying the ideas) and how to combine the two to innovate. They were trained in the use of different creative tools and used them practically, and, finally, the students reflected on the results they reached and the neurological causes of both successes and failures. The scientists themselves use the process of learning how to drive as a metaphor for the process the students went through. To learn how to drive a car, you must first have a basic understanding of how a car works and how to move in traffic (the theory). You don't need to be an expert, but you need to have a fairly good understanding of the basics. Next, you need to learn to apply the theory in practice, but under supervision (driving with a driving instructor). After a certain period of training, you are ready to be released into traffic and to train yourself to reach expert level driving.

Maybe it's just me, but when I think of the above exemplification, which uses driving as an analogy for the process of acquiring new skills, it sounds banal. First, you need to understand how things work, and the better you understand the underlying mechanisms, the better equipped you are to do it yourself. Next, you need to learn to use them in practice with help, and finally you are ready to do it yourself. But the description is banal because it's true. It is precisely the way people learn and the way people best develop their creativity. It is not only documented in Friis-Olivarius and Onarheim's research, but also through a meta-analysis of more than 70 creativity training studies.[10]

The point is that we don't teach our children to maintain their creativity in school, nor do we teach our employees to use their creativity and their divergent thinking faculties in our organizations. Instead, we cultivate convergent thinking, the ability to criticize and qualify, which is also crucial for innovation processes, but the emphasis is not equal on both thinking modes. We put too much emphasis on critical thinking and too little emphasis on creative thinking.

There are actually simple tools for developing creative skills and for (re)instructing people, and therefore also organizations, to be innovative. You can test your own skills relatively easily, and you can establish some processes to develop your organization's innovation power to include both the conversion of development processes to agile methods and the implementation of different innovation processes, which we will examine more closely in the section on the element of process. But before we reach that point, it is important to understand the psychology behind what it takes for your employees to create maximum value and thrive in their working environment.

In 2012, Google launched a research study with approximately 200 teams that they followed for several years to learn what creates consistently successful teams. Not teams that succeed with initiatives every now and then, but teams that are consistently successful. The project was named Project Aristotle[11], and it generated some interesting and surprising results. It turned out that when the analysts looked at parameters such as the composition of introverts and extroverts in a team, educational background, tenure, hierarchical positions, and past successes, there was no correlation between them and the current teams' success rates. However, through in-depth observations of how teams work together, interviews to understand the team members' experiences, analyses of the language they used to describe their experiences, different experiments where teams were to solve specific tasks together, and statistical analyses, the analysts found some interesting results.

The absolute most crucial parameter for creating consistently successful teams proved to be psychological safety. A conclusion that Harvard professor Amy Edmondson also reached in a study that she conducted in 1999[12], where she studied team dynamics of 51 different teams in a production company, and which Google researchers subsequently compared their findings to, in order to fully understand their own observations. Psychological safety is a term describing the feeling that you can express your opinions without being put down for it; that you are heard and able to speak your mind when you feel it's relevant; that there is a flat hierarchy in which everyone, including the boss, respects you; and that the manager has a coaching approach to management. Hence, you feel it is safe to take risks, which is an absolute necessity for creating innovation and development. According to Anders Mortensen, a director at Google, they have actually measured that teams that feel psychologically safe overperform on the company's established goals, while teams that don't feel psychologically safe underperform.

Project Aristotle also revealed that reliability (ensuring team members adhere to their agreements), structure and clarity (knowing their role, plans, and goals), meaning (finding that your work is meaningful) and impact (that you feel that your work has a greater societal significance) are crucial parameters,[13] but psychological safety was the most crucial factor for high-performing teams.

Google's study also indicates that the specific individuals who are part of a team matters less than how a team is together. This might make you think that who you hire isn't so important, but that's certainly not what Google thinks. How you collaborate may be more important than who you collaborate with, but who you're working with still matters. Therefore, Google also has extremely thorough recruitment procedures. In addition to having the privilege that many people want to work for them, which means that there are always several qualified candidates to choose from, all future employees will be interviewed by at least four different people, who all, independently of each other, need to agree that an applicant has the right profile for employment. An added frill worth mentioning is that, as a leader at

Google, you are not necessarily part of the hiring process of your own employees. Many leaders I have encountered have reacted to that approach with disbelief and nervous tics. But at Google, the argument is that employees are not hired to create value in a department; they are hired to create value throughout the company, and therefore, a leader doesn't need to be part of the process of employing the people who will work in their specific department. At Google, future employees are assessed on their general cognitive capabilities, i.e. the ability to solve problems, the knowledge related to the position to be filled, and the difficult-to-define 'Googliness' that means whether or not you fit with the culture.

Many companies are increasingly aiming to employ with diversity in mind, and here we enter into truly controversial territories, where Google has been attacked many times for being too dominated by a culture of white men, although Google was among the first globally listed companies to publish data on their diversity metrics.[14] But is diversity really important for a company's results? Is it a company's responsibility to ensure that its employees are evenly distributed across genders, races, cultures, and ages? And does it make any difference at all?

If you speak to the Norwegian diversity expert Isabelle Ringnes, who, among others, started TENK (Technology Network for Women) and the organization #ShesGotThis, which aims to create valid methods for increasing gender diversity in organizations, there is no doubt that there is a gender diversity problem in most companies. 'There are as many CEOs in Norway named Arne as there are female CEOs in total,' she says to emphasize how low the percentage of female top executives is. In the US the equivalent is John and David. There are more CEOs named John and David than there are women CEOs.[15] A major experiment, conducted in both the United States and Norway, emphasizes the point. About 20 years ago in Harvard, a number of students were asked to read a case about a well-known venture capitalist from Silicon Valley,[16] who invested in startups. The students were to read the case and then evaluate the investor on a number of parameters such as competence and their willingness to work with the person. However, the experiment was designed in such a way that half the students read a case where the person they were to evaluate was Heidi Roizen, while the other half read exactly the same case in which the protagonist was named Howard Roizen. The evaluations of the investors proved to be widely different. Howard and Heidi were deemed equally competent by the students, but Howard was considered to be a more attractive colleague to work with, while Heidi was deemed to be too selfish and to be a less attractive colleague. The exact same study was conducted in 2015 in Norway, the second most equal country in the world, with the same results.[17] The experiments point to the fact that there are some fundamental biases against women as leaders, even among young people and in the most equal countries in the world.

At the same time, various studies show that there are clear economic and innovation benefits to having women in executive leadership. A survey by the Boston Consulting Group from 2017 suggests that the most gender-diverse companies have 38% higher profits from new innovations than other companies.[18] Another study by the consulting firm EY looked at results from more than 21,000 global public companies and found that companies with at least 30% women in leadership positions had a 6% better bottom line.[19] A third study that analysed gender distribution in research and development teams in more than 4000 Spanish companies found that companies with more women in these teams introduced more radical innovations over a two-year period.[20]

Venture capitalist Paul Gompers has investigated thousands of investment cases[21] to reveal the potential influence of diversity on the results of US investment companies that are characteristically extremely homogeneous. Only 8% of the investors are women, and 1 and 2% are of African-American or Latin-American descent, respectively. Even in terms of investors' typical educational backgrounds, there was a clear bias in favour of colleagues from their own educational background, as there was a 34.4% higher probability that investors would work together if they were educated at the same schools. However, diversity was a positive influence, both in terms of the profitability of individual investments and the overall results of investment companies. Acquisitions and IPOs (when companies are publicly traded on the stock market) had an 11.5% lower success rate at investment firms where the partners had the same educational background and, in racially homogeneous backgrounds, the negative effect was all the way up to 26.4–32.2%. Gompers' analyses showed that the high level of homogeneity was a weakness when investors contributed to the strategy or the recruitment of employees to the companies they invested in. This means that a lack of diversity made for poorer consultancy because there was a lack of variety in the input that investors contributed.

On the basis of these studies, you could ask yourself how come there is such a diversity problem when analyses show that excessive homogeneity negatively affects the bottom line. According to Isabelle Ringnes, it is mainly due to the lack of awareness of the problem. Many people think that they are open and inclusive, even though they aren't due to their unconscious biases. This also applies in my own area of the world, the Nordic countries, where the communities are very homogeneous.

Secondly, it is due to the fact that companies working to ensure more diversity often launch initiatives based on their assumptions rather than on analyses. There is a lot of research on the problem, but very little research on solutions. Therefore, companies often make mistakes and launch initiatives that don't work. According to a report from McKinsey, only 16% of businesses are actively involved in strengthening gender balance.[22] Therefore, Isabelle Ringnes recommends that you create an ambassador's body in your organization, which helps gain insight into the issue, establishes fact-based dialogue, and from there ensures that there are concrete ambitious goals for actions taken to solve the problem. This is what the Norwegian bank DNB has done. Here, the board demanded that the company had a minimum of 60/40 gender distribution at all levels of the organization, created role model programmes and guaranteed equal pay, and ensured that there was always a man and a woman to choose between in connection with recruitment and career planning.

When it comes to different forms of diversity in companies besides gender, be it race, culture, or age, there are far fewer studies that have explored the effects of diversity, even though there are also signs that diversity within these parameters affects companies' bottom lines and innovation power. The above-mentioned study done in investment companies is one of the exceptions. But an English study with over 7000 companies also showed that companies with greater cultural diversity in management also developed more new products, making them more innovative.[23]

Basically, there is a lack of diversity in many companies. This is true for startups and for established organizations. There is talk of 'bromance cultures' in startups, which is not only a Silicon Valley phenomenon, but one that is also found in startup companies in Europe. Most startups are as a result extremely male-dominated; they primarily hire white – typically young – men, and these white young men either deliberately or subconsciously prefer to hire more white young men. The established organizations don't have a bromance problem; they have an 'old-white-men' problem, and the higher up in the hierarchies you reach, the older and whiter the people tend to get. There are no easy answers here. Raising awareness of this problem is the first step, and the next is to establish measurable processes to move your organization towards more diversity. It's a long tough process. But there is no excuse for not doing it. There's a lot that speaks for the fact that diversity strengthens innovation and the bottom line. But even if that were not the case, the morally right thing to do is to ensure that our organizations reflect our societal contexts and ensure inclusion of everyone, regardless of sex, age, race, and culture.

Processes That Strengthen Innovation Culture

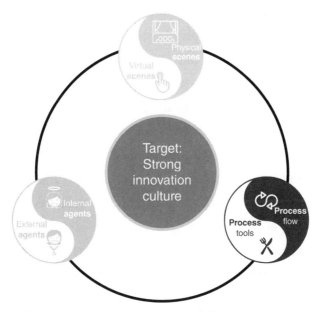

Model 4   Elements to Enhance Innovation Culture

In the same way that the physical and digital scenes are important tools for hacking the culture and creating a stronger innovation culture, and that the agents (primarily in terms of people) have a major influence on companies' culture and results, the processes used are crucial. Processes, as mentioned earlier, consist of the workflow you have and the tools that you use for them. In other words, processes are about the way things are done.

Some companies have experimented with how long you can concentrate before your productivity and creativity drops and which processes can be optimized to boost output. A few years ago, when I translated the book *Exponential Organizations* from English to Danish, which required a high degree of concentration, it became clear to me that after about 45 minutes of work, I became noticeably worse at the task and that even simple words and sentences became harder for me to translate. If I simply took a five-minute break, I had renewed energy and was able to, once again, work at a much higher-quality level.

In Denmark, the IT company IIH Nordic has taken the principle of short breaks seriously and, after a three-year test period, they have radically changed their workflow with the pomodoro technique as a key tool. According to this technique, you work in short 25-minute blocks, while ensuring zero interruptions during that time. After 25 minutes, you have to take a break to do something relaxing and unrelated to work. Then you can continue with the next 25-minute work block. For many, working for such brief periods of time will sound intuitively wrong, and it will sound like completing all your tasks would be more difficult. The point of the system is that you work in a very concentrated way, without interruptions and in a time interval that equals the duration for which most people are able to deliver high-quality performance before losing concentration.[24] According to Henrik Stenmann, IIH Nordic's CEO, the introduction of the pomodoro technique, along with a focus on healthier meals in the canteen and a reduction in working time from 37 to 30 weekly hours (they have Fridays off), resulted in a productivity increase of 20%, a halving of absence due to illness, and an increase in the company's so-called 'wellness score' by 70%.[25]

'Agile' is another buzzword that you should know as it's not just used to blow hot air: it actually refers to a valuable methodology that can lead to radically better results than traditional project management and development tools. Originally, agile was developed as a method for software companies. Software is constantly being upgraded – what we know as versions 2.0. The agile concept is no longer used exclusively by software companies and IT departments, but is increasingly being implemented across departments in established companies. The origin of the method can be dated back to 2001, when the 'Manifesto for Agile Software Development' was published.[26] The manifesto was written by a group of frustrated software developers who were tired of never being able to adhere to budgets and schedules, and who had developed a number of principles to ensure that things could be done easier and faster. According to McKinsey's agile experts, 46% of IT projects exceed their budget and 33% are not completed on time.[27] In other words, there is room for improvement and agile could be the solution. The manifesto grossly described the philosophy of the new processes as follows: to value individuals and collaboration over processes and tools, functional software over extensive documentation, customer collaboration over contract negotiations, and responsiveness to changes over sticking to the plan.[28] So agile is an experimental approach with ongoing development and evaluation, where you also work closely with customers to create the best end result, which is radically different from the traditional waterfall method, where you try to predict the end result and describe all the (often year-long) processes, before work is commenced. In a rapidly changing world with accelerating technological development, agile is looking like a far more logical methodology, which, thanks to its experimental approach, boosts the innovation power of organizations.

Take a company like the Danish–Swedish dairy giant Arla Foods that is the leading dairy product manufacturer in the Nordic region. They have begun their journey towards augmenting the organization and strengthening the innovation culture by experimenting with so-called agile sprints, i.e. short, focused development processes, in IT. Initially, they completed a single project to learn how it worked, they gained experience from the experiment, and then decided to roll it out across the entire IT organization and use agile sprints on all new projects. Arla Foods has, among other things, worked with their ability to predict milk production from the thousands of farmers who supply dairies, which by its very nature is a decisive ability if you want to optimize the production equipment. By working with data from farmers via newly developed machine-learning algorithms, improving scenario analyses, and establishing so-called forecasting dashboards, Arla Foods optimized their prediction skills from 60 to 97.4% over a very short period of time. The project alone added extra millions to the bottom line. After 1.5 years, Arla Foods IT therefore made agile sprints the standard process for all new projects. The number of releases was raised from two to ten per year, the time from commencement to project delivery was halved, and work satisfaction was increased as employees thought it was more fun to work dynamically with far quicker results than with the waterfall method's very costly and time-consuming documentation and control processes. A core group from IT has now been tasked with helping the rest of the organization learn the same methods.

You could say that the agile methodology hacks the culture and raises the innovation force because the experimental approach causes everyone involved to bring their personal innovation power to the table. And the very idea of making every organization member a co-creator in innovation is a key element in creating a culture full of incremental innovators.

That was software company Cisco's philosophy when they introduced the Innovate Everywhere Challenge,[29] aimed at engaging all employees in an idea contest and developing concepts which had the potential of becoming concrete services. More than half of their 72,000-strong workforce took part in the first year of the competition. Put briefly, employees were asked to develop solutions with the help of other forces in the organization that could act as mentors and contribute with expertise. The best ideas received $25,000 each, enabling employees to work on, and concretize, the ideas.

At Unilever, efforts have been made to strengthen the innovation force in the supply chain by establishing a mini accelerator[30] called 'Digifunds'. Here, the employees have been invited to submit ideas for supply chain improvements that could be implemented for 10,000 euros or less. So, small innovations. The call was super-simple: submit a maximum four-minute long video, answer three questions, and after 48 hours, you'll be informed whether or not you will get the money to develop the idea. Of the ideas suggested by the employees, 70% were supported and implemented. This initiative may sound like a very small and insignificant effort, and there are, of course, limits to how much value projects such as mini-accelerators can generate in relation to the development of new innovations. There is no way it could serve as a company's sole approach to creating a strong innovation culture. But it can at least do two things: optimize the likelihood of harvesting low-hanging fruits, which there would otherwise be no motivation to address, and train employees to think in a development and solution-oriented way.

NNIT, a leading Danish provider of IT services and consulting services, has chosen an even more ambitious model known
as BIG (Business Innovation Growth) to strengthen the innovation culture in the core organization. The programme was
established based on the observation that an additional innovation machine was needed to explore and test new ideas faster
than they could with their current Stage Gate model. In the BIG
programme, a team can win a pot of money, which they get
three months to spend on testing an idea and building a Minimum Viable Product (MVP). The money is primarily used to
buy internal resources 'free', but also covers expenses like hardware, software, or other expenses that a startup might have.

The first BIG team was appointed through an open competition, where all employees had the opportunity to offer ideas.
Out of these ideas, 14 were chosen to be presented in a kind of
Dragon's Den where the idea people pitched their ideas and a
select BIG jury had the opportunity to vote for them. Five ideas
went on to a pitch to senior management, and the winners were
awarded the money and the three months for further development. For NNIT, it was important that the project be physically
implemented in the organization itself, so that the team would be
close to the resources they needed. But it was, at the same time,
also important that a new innovation space was established,
where the team could move in for three months – thereby moving away from their usual offices in order to work on the project

outside of day-to-day operations. Some team members worked on the assignment full-time, while others only used 80% of their time, and the aim from the beginning was that whatever they developed could be translated into business value for the organization within three months.

According to NNIT's Chief Technology Officer, Jens Maagøe, the purpose is about ensuring that a founder mentality is allowed to grow among the company's employees. And that seems to be a smart idea, as analyses indicate that companies with a founder mentality generate three times better results for their shareholders than companies without, because they maintain the entrepreneurial features that characterize newly established businesses and limit bureaucracy.[31] Another secondary effect is that the initiative has positively affected the rest of the organization. Employees find it fun and exciting to work in a company that takes such initiatives.

Internal communication is another overlooked process tool, despite the fact that most companies of a certain size have communications departments that can influence the culture using simple tools. In the global consultancy firm KPMG, an interesting project was carried out that focused on strengthening the shared experience of the company through communication. However, the principle in this process can equally be translated into the work of strengthening the shared experience of innovation. The project was called 'The 10,000 Stories-Challenge'. The aim was to make the connection between the company's purpose and the daily work of the employees visible. Employees were therefore encouraged to illustrate how they themselves helped make a difference in the form of posters (using a design programme provided by the company), which described the value that the individual employee created in the company. They were encouraged to come up with a headline that illustrated the value they felt that they created, and its connection with their job duties. One example was a poster with the heading 'I fight terrorism', and the descriptive text highlighted how they worked to ensure that companies couldn't launder money. In order to push the process and ensure a greater degree of involvement, management promised two additional vacation days if they could quickly produce 10,000 posters. That goal was significantly exceeded. In total, 27,000 employees produced 42,000 posters,[32] and most importantly, employees' pride in their work and their sense of contributing significantly increased. Again, we see a simple hack that barely costs anything, and yet it significantly influences the culture that is desired in a company.

Other communication processes that have a major influence on innovation culture are things like town hall meetings for the entire company, where management informs, and engages in dialogue with, the employees. Google holds 'Thank God

It's Friday' Town Halls every week, where the entire company globally meets, both physically and virtually, to be briefed by senior management and everyone gets the opportunity to ask questions. If you are a senior executive, how often do you meet all your employees and brief them on ongoing activities and interact with them? Or if you are not a senior executive, how often do you have the opportunity to enter into dialogue with senior management? In many companies, it may be once a year in connection with financial statements, or when new transformation projects are announced. Or never. Holding weekly meetings ensures transparency and cohesion in the organization, and it signals how important it is considered to involve employees at all levels in the company's future.

In Amazon, you don't produce long PowerPoints to sell your ideas to management. Instead, you write an essay of a maximum of six pages. I had the pleasure of discussing culture hacks with a high-ranking employee at Amazon who told me about this process and about how intimidating it was to write such an essay the first time. The principle behind the six-page essay is that the sender gets to the point and is as concise as possible. French philosopher Blaise Pascal has had these words attributed to him: 'I have made this one (letter) longer than usual because I have not had time to make it shorter.'[33] It is much more difficult to express yourself succinctly than the opposite. In many places, weeks and months are spent developing endless

PowerPoints with dense bullet points and complicated process diagrams to sell ideas to management. It just doesn't work, as it's usually difficult to understand the purpose of such documents, even for management, and many good projects end up on the cutting floor because they are poorly communicated. By making the format both short and detailed, and because you are forced to write in full sentences, you also have to consider every single word, every single sentence and every single argument. At the same time, a meeting participant usually shouldn't prepare for such a meeting at Amazon. They meet up, receive the printed essay, read it through with a red pen, write down their comments on the paper and discuss it with the essay writer. The man who told me about the process described the situation as being similar to a schoolboy doing an exam with five examiners. But the method works. It is effective and precise.

While Amazon consciously uses the technology of the past, namely paper, Airbus has, together with Singularity University, experimented with the technology of the future to strengthen communication, learning, and culture.[34] Together, the two parties developed what they called mixed reality training. They used Microsoft HoloLens, which is a mix of virtual reality and augmented reality glasses that employees could put on and thereby participate in a virtual aerodynamic training programme. Based on the experiment, Airbus established a holo academy with the purpose of developing more of these types of training efforts. Because of the higher degree of involvement you experience when using virtual and augmented reality, you actually learn better, because it involves kinaesthetic learning. At the same time, the use of new technology has the secondary effect that employees feel that they are working in an innovative company, precisely because of the use of new technology, which sends a strong signal about a focus on future innovations.

Other Cultural Hacks

There is a long list of other cultural hacks that can be implemented to strengthen your innovation culture. I briefly discuss some of them below. Most of these examples do not come from 100-year-old established organizations, but from younger digital companies. Nevertheless, they are worth looking to for inspiration. And the good thing is that they are all super-simple and virtually cost nothing. However, these culture hacks are far from easy to implement; they require both motivation and persistence. Somebody needs to take the lead and insist on completing the projects, and to persist the fifth, sixth, and seventh time that not everyone is excited about the new initiative. But if you succeed with your efforts, it has a huge impact on the culture you create.

- – ING, the big Dutch bank, founded the first digital bank back in the 1990s. I recently had the pleasure of having lunch with a senior executive from that time and asked him what the biggest barrier he experienced was when ING founded the digital bank. He replied that it was jealousy in the old part of the bank. 'How can it be that we, as an organization, are spending a lot of money establishing new strange units when I have to go and save money in my part of the company?' the employees asked him, 'and on top of that, we are the ones who make the money to fund the new experiments'. But by circulating employees from the old part of the organization into the new part as a kind of internship, the company managed to reduce the levels of jealousy. What happened was a demystification of what was happening in the new unit, and the old employees were taught new tricks that they could take with them into the established part of the organization.

– The energy company Ørsted uses the same principle and circulates its graduates, the newly hired young employees, through several departments in their two-year graduate programme, to ensure that the young people gain a broad understanding of the company and create networks across it. It strengthens the innovation power.

– Amazon is one of the masters of cultural hacks. In addition to the six-page essay, they are also known for the pizza rule for team composition. The pizza rule means that you should never put together a team so big that it can't be fed by two pizzas. The more people in a team, the more complicated communication becomes and, according to Amazon, this impedes execution and innovation.[35] At Space10, IKEA's external accelerator, they say that you should never have more than five people in a team because the complexity of possible communication routes increases significantly with each new person.

– Amazon has also invented the institutional 'yes', which means that if a boss rejects a project idea from an employee, they should write a two-page-long argument about why they've said no and publish it on the intranet. With this rule, a boss thinks twice before saying no,[36] giving the idea the attention it deserves.

– X, Alphabet's Moonshot Factory – which is what they call the laboratory where they developed self-driving cars, Google Glass, and many other radical innovations – has an interesting way of acknowledging results. They hand out what they call 'The Get Weird Award'. The prize is given to the teams who choose to explore the strangest or most unconventional hypothesis. The remarkable thing here is, however, that the prize is awarded before the team completes the experiment. Because the prize is not awarded for the experiment's results. It is given for having the courage to dare explore the unobvious. This principle can also be used in connection with less radical innovations.[37] Based on a similar principle, the Indian conglomerate Tata distributes a 'Dare to Try' prize to individuals or teams whose projects teach the organization something about things that don't work.[38]

– The marketing software company HubSpot holds 'mystery dinners' where different people from the company who do not know each other are put together to share a meal somewhere in the city. The purpose is to bring together people who don't usually talk with each other to strengthen relationships across the organization. The same company sponsors meals between employees. As an employee, you can petition your immediate supervisor to pay for dinner with a colleague you don't know but want to get to know. As we know, food is amazingly stimulating for conversation, and through this simple and inexpensive method, HubSpot motivates employees to get to know each other across the organization, which promotes innovation.[39]

– The file storage company Dropbox holds an annual hackathon for all its employees. Not just for the programmers or the innovation department. The whole organization, as a result, is helping the company's development and continuously training its innovation power.[40]

– In the new CEO Satya Nadella's first year as chief executive, Microsoft also used hackathons to send an internal signal that the organization wanted to enhance its innovation culture by inviting more than 12,000 employees from 83 countries to a hackathon in its headquarters.[41]

– IBM in the Nordic region holds reverse mentor sessions, where senior executives shadow young employees for a half to a whole day to understand them better and to create a stronger culture.[42] Based on the same principle, my company often runs reverse mentor sessions between executives from established organizations and startups, where it is the startup people who advise the established players on how to work with new business models, technologies, and management styles.

– Salesforce has what they call the 1-1-1 model, which means they donate 1% of their annual results, 1% of their software, and 1% of their employees' time to charitable causes. As a result, employees can take time to work on special projects, entirely outside the Salesforce domain, without compromising their wages or career opportunities. This contributes to motivating employees, giving them the feeling that the company is driven with a purpose, and giving them new input that ultimately strengthens innovation power.[43]

– More and more companies are setting up so-called academies where they regularly organize lectures and courses, where all employees can get inspiration and further training on topics that are both directly work-related and focused on personal development. Even when courses are not directly work-related, there is a secondary benefit for businesses, because acquiring new knowledge and inspiration outside your personal normal area of competence strengthens the brain's capacity for divergent thinking and, thus, creativity.

– In my company, we have dedicated resources to enable all employees to spend working hours on coaching sessions with a professional coach where they can discuss anything. The purpose is to give them a space where they can explore ideas and consider questions that are important to them. We therefore help employees find their true motivations, even if it turns out that a coaching session helps them realize that they shouldn't work for our business anymore. We've based this initiative on a philosophy that can be illustrated by the meme you have probably seen on LinkedIn, where a CFO says: 'What if we spend money on training our employees and they leave us?' to the CEO, to which the CEO replies: 'What if we don't, and they stay?'

– Maersk Growth, Maersk's venture arm, which we return to, has set up a 'culture club' that investigates what kind of culture employees want, and how they establish cohesion with the Maersk organization's set of values. The company also holds 'growth corners', which are half-day events, where employees can pitch new ideas, experts are invited to hold talks, or you can take the microphone and talk about what's on your mind. Here, you can also invite colleagues from the parent organization. Finally, they hold 'fish bowls' – a method where you set up four chairs, put three people in the chairs who want to contribute with their views on the theme of the day – themes include culture or how best to give feedback – and alternately take a chair when you want to share your opinion.

NOTES

1. George Land & Beth Jarman, Breakpoint and Beyond: Mastering the Future—Today, 1993.
2. www.designcouncil.org.uk/sites/default/files/asset/document/impact-office-design-full-research.pdf.
3. Banbury, S. and Berry, D., Disruption of office-related tasks by speech and office noise, 1998.
4. www.designcouncil.org.uk/sites/default/files/asset/document/impact-office-design-full-research.pdf.
5. www.designcouncil.org.uk/sites/default/files/asset/document/impact-office-design-full-research.pdf.
6. http://pinnacle-secure.allenpress.com/doi/full/10.22361/jfmer/76637?code=SASU-site.
7. https://adobe99u.files.wordpress.com/2013/07/2010%2Bjep%2Bspace%2Bexperiments.pdf.
8. Anthony Brandt & David Eagleman, The Runaway Species, 2017.
9. www.ncbi.nlm.nih.gov/pmc/articles/PMC3797545.
10. Scott G., Leritz L.E., Mumford, M.D. (2004). The effectiveness of creativity training: a quantitative review. *Creat. Res. J.* 16, 361–388 10.1080/10400410409534549.
11. www.nytimes.com/2016/02/28/magazine/what-google-learned-from-its-quest-to-build-the-perfect-team.html.
12. Amy Edmondson, Psychological Safety and Learning Behavior in Work Teams, *Administrative Science Quarterly,* Vol. 44, No. 2 (Jun., 1999), pp. 350–383, Published by Sage Publications, Inc., on behalf of the Johnson Graduate School of Management, Cornell University.
13. https://rework.withgoogle.com/print/guides/5721312655835136.
14. https://www.pbs.org/newshour/nation/google-discloses-workforce-diversity-data-good.
15. www.nytimes.com/2015/03/03/upshot/fewer-women-run-big-companies-than-men-named-john.html.
16. https://hbr.org/2013/03/three-reasons-men-should-read.

17. www.tankesmienagenda.no/wp-content/uploads/Tankesmien-Agenda-Rapport-Menn-som-ikke-liker-karrierekvinner.pdf.
18. BCG, The Most Innovative Companies 2016.
19. www.linkedin.com/pulse/why-organizations-led-women-perform-better-jeppe-vilstrup-hansgaard/?trackingId=xWqrj3HA572oGSB9uHt qQA%3D%3D.
20. https://hbr.org/2016/11/why-diverse-teams-are-smarter.
21. https://hbr.org/2018/07/the-other-diversity-dividend?utm _campaign=hbr&utm_medium=social&u.
22. https://www.mckinsey.com/~/media/mckinsey/business% 20functions/organization/our%20insights/delivering%20through% 20diversity/delivering-through-diversity_full-report.ashx.
23. https://www.tandfonline.com/doi/abs/10.1111/ecge.12016.
24. Francesco Cirillo, The Pomodoro Technique: The Life-Changing Time Management System, 2017.
25. www.business.dk/digital/arbejdsuge-paa-fire-dage-dansk-virksomhed-har-oeget-produktiviteten-og.
26. http://agilemanifesto.org/.
27. https://www.mckinsey.com/business-functions/organization/our-insights/agile-with-a-capital-a-a-guide-to-the-principles-and-pitfalls-of-agile-development.
28. http://agilemanifesto.org/.
29. https://innov8rs.co/news/make-innovation-part-everyones-job-cisco-ge-adobe-intuit-intrapreneurship.
30. www.supplychainquarterly.com/news/20180604-how-unilever-funds-supply-chain-innovation/.
31. https://hbr.org/2016/12/when-large-companies-are-better-at-entrepreneurship-than-startups.
32. https://hbr.org/2015/10/how-an-accounting-firm-convinced-its-employees-they-could-change-the-world.
33. https://quoteinvestigator.com/2012/04/28/shorter-letter.
34. www.nextbigfuture.com/2017/11/singularity-university-partners-with-airbus-on-mixed-reality-training.html.

35. www.theguardian.com/technology/2018/apr/24/the-two-pizza-rule-and-the-secret-of-amazons-success.
36. Salim Ismail et al., Exponential Organizations, 2014.
37. Peter Diamandis & Steven Kotler, Bold, 2015.
38. Anthony Brandt & David Eagleman, The Runaway Species, 2017.
39. https://tech.co/company-culture-of-hubspot-2013-04.
40. www.theverge.com/2014/7/24/5930927/why-dropbox-gives-its-employees-a-week-to-do-whatever-they-want.
41. Satya Nadella et al., Hit Refresh, 2017.
42. www.computerworld.dk/art/243920/for-at-vaere-sikre-paa-at-vi-forstaar-vores-unge-medarbejdere-har-vi-vendt-det-om-saa-jeg-og-andre-ledere-gaar-jeg-som-foel-hos-dem-i-en-halv-til-hel-dag#BVUtAehWXVe5VlcA.99.
43. www.salesforce.com/company/ventures/pledge1.

CHAPTER 12

CAN YOU IMAGINE A FUTURE THAT DOESN'T INVOLVE X?: MUTATING INNOVATION

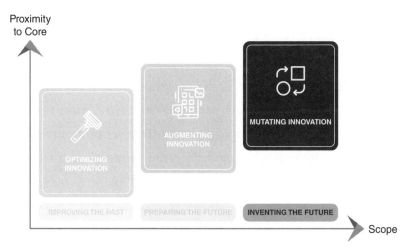

Model 3   Overview of the three innovation tracks
Source: Kris Østergaard

When asked about the timeline for when the first space elevator would be built, Arthur C. Clarke, the world-famous author who wrote the science fiction book *2001: A Space Odyssey* and the first person to describe how satellites could be used to create global communications networks,[1] replied: 'probably 50 years after they all stop laughing'.

The quote was, in fact, not Arthur C. Clarke's. He borrowed it from another visionary Arthur, namely the American scientist and engineer Arthur Kantrowitz, who also researched space travel and inspired Clarke's description of space elevators moving from the ground and rising 36,000 km into space[2] in the novel *The Fountains of Paradise*. The quote holds a greater truth, with which many visionary inventors and scientists agree. Ideas and concepts that challenge existing paradigms will often be ridiculed and deemed impossible by both experts and laymen, until it is obvious that they are no longer impossible.

From Alexander Graham Bell's telephone patent, which the American communications company Western Union refused to buy for $100,000, to John Logie Baird's invention of the first television, which was rejected by radio pioneers as an insignificant invention,[3] to the Wright brothers' plane, Ford's mass produced car, and the well-known rejections of personal computers, cell phones, electric cars, self-driving cars and so on. . . rejection and ridicule are the most frequent responses to radical inventions that challenge mainstream products. But as history has shown us, never say never, as long as the ideas don't violate the laws of physics, and be careful with rejecting possibilities just because they challenge what currently exists. On the contrary, you should ensure that, in your organization, it is possible to experiment with precisely the technologies and business models that challenge your own core business, because this is the only way to ensure your long-term success.

Thus, at the time of writing this, there are also signs that space elevators have moved one step closer to realization. The Japanese Shizuoka University and the Japanese space agency, Japan Aerospace Exploration Agency, have announced that they are working to conduct an experiment in space, where they will be the first in the world to try to prove that space elevators[4] are feasible. Sure, there is only talk of a 3 x 3 x 6 cm elevator-like object that will move along a 10-metre long cable, which is stretched between two mini-satellites. But if the experiment succeeds, it would serve as proof of concept that space elevators are feasible. Another Japanese organization, the construction company Obayashi Corporation, which is also behind one of the highest observatory towers in the world – Tokyo Skytree at 634 metres[5] – estimates that they can build a space elevator by 2050, provided that carbon nanotubes, the crucial building material which would make the elevator cables strong enough, can be produced in sufficient quantities by 2030.[6] And now, this is even more likely to happen because researchers at the Chinese Tsinghua University are working intensively to enable mass production of the carbon nanotubes developed by its scientists, which is so strong that a cubic centimetre can withstand masses of more than up to 800 tons.[7] In other words, there are a lot of people in Japan and China who have stopped laughing, and it pays to shelve arrogance and to thoroughly investigate the options before reflexively rejecting them. This is precisely how radical experiments lead to mutating innovations.

Mutating innovation is the third innovation track that has been referenced a few times throughout the book. This is where you're no longer improving the past, as with optimizing innovation, or preparing the future, as with augmenting innovation, but where you invent the future. Put in another way, you're no longer upgrading the core; you're challenging the core with the purpose of identifying which significant, nonlinear innovations you can create to future-proof the organization in the long term.

In Chapter 3, which explored the question 'Which industry am I in?' we used Amazon as an example of a company that continuously mutates both through its own experiments and through its acquisitions. The principle is embedded in the company's DNA, but is quite unique to Amazon. Only a few companies operate in the same way. In fact, analyses show that there are currently fewer companies that have teams dedicated to exploring new technology than years back.[8] And mutating innovation is a difficult discipline. Because most companies are in situations where they lack the resources needed to challenge the core. Because if you're going to challenge your organization's existing core, it requires another breed of people, namely the radical innovators we identified earlier; it requires new capabilities; insight into new technologies; the development of new business models; and an attitude which is open to experimenting with the unknown, where you simply cannot prepare a business case. All of this is contrary to conventional wisdom in most organizations.

Therefore, you must also physically move away from the core organization when you initiate and run such initiatives. This is sometimes called 'innovation on the edges'. Because the initiatives will not have a chance at succeeding within the core. It will be too noisy, as initiatives challenge what currently exists, i.e. precisely the things that the majority of the organization's employees are working to optimize or augment. As an employee, you are either working to optimize or upgrade what currently exists (optimizing or augmenting innovation), or you are working to challenge it (mutating innovation). You can't do both at the same time. The conflict of interest is too big. So when you hear managers say to employees within the core organization that they must disrupt themselves, it basically means that they should start sawing off the branch they are sitting on. It can't succeed. They are, after all, working to stabilize that branch every day. So instead of asking employees within the core organization to disrupt themselves and saw off their own branch, take other employees away from the core and plant new trees.

Fortunately, there are also a number of functional tools that forward-looking organizations are using, and which we will now look at more closely. This is especially about the establishment of X divisions, sometimes called innovation labs or skunk works; partnerships; establishment of brand new companies; and radical open innovation. And when challenging the core, as is the case with mutating innovation, you need to demonstrate what you want to achieve with visions. This is best done through a reverse engineering design process where you travel from the future back to the present.

BACK TO THE PRESENT

Space projects are exciting to use as inspiration for more earthbound efforts, because if you want to travel into space, you need to have visionary glasses on. It is, per definition, incredibly difficult, and no one has typically done anything like it before, so there are a lot of wheels to invent. Besides the efforts of the Americans throughout the 1960s, and the efforts of the billionaire club Musk, Bezos, and Branson in the 2000s and 2010s, few have demonstrated such a dedicated desire to occupy space as the Japanese. The Japanese interest in space has resulted in the creation of the startup iSpace,[9] which in 2018 raised about $80 million to become the first privately owned company licensed to send a rocket to the Moon using micro-robotics, i.e. small cheap self-propelled units. The time horizon for this initiative is not 10, 15, or 20 years. In the second quarter of 2020, iSpace plans to sends the first rocket into orbit around the Moon. In the second quarter of 2021, they plan to land on the Moon and send out small vehicles to search for water. But the goal of iSpace is not just sending a private rocket to the Moon and looking for water. The goal is to make the Earth and the Moon a cohesive ecosystem where the Moon contributes resources to the Earth, and, therefore, to build a city with 1000 inhabitants and 10,000 annual visitors by the end of 2040.

In other words, there is a big vision behind the project, and as Kyle Acierno, the managing director of iSpace in Europe, told me, you, of course, don't 'just' build a new city on the Moon. It's a big and complicated project, which is further complicated by the fact that iSpace doesn't yet know exactly how to build a city on the Moon, and doesn't yet have the technologies to complete the project. There is much they have yet to learn about how to make it possible. Therefore, they work with a reverse engineering design strategy. That is to say, they have set the long-term goal of establishing a city on the Moon in 2040, and then they have identified which interim goals they need to achieve to make it possible to work backwards into the present. In other words, if there is to be a city on the Moon in 2040, an industrial platform must first be built that allows for construction projects on the Moon; and to make this possible, a variety of tools need to be transported to the moon, including 3D printers that can print buildings; and to make this possible, there must first be water on the Moon, so that you know where the city is to be established, as water is vital to life; and to make this possible, vehicles must first be sent out on the Moon to search for water; and to make this possible, a rocket must first be sent to the Moon; and to make this possible, a rocket must first be sent into orbit. And in this way, exemplified here in a very simplified form, we are back to mission 1, which will be completed in 2020 and is being prepared now.

Very few companies work in this way. Most work in the short term and build on the present, and then they make projections a few quarters into the future. Partly because they don't have big enough visions, partly because they dare not engage in projects for which they don't have most of the answers before commencing. I have also cheated a bit now, because I have used iSpace as an example, a relatively newly established company, and as I said before, newer companies have a much easier time with innovation than large well-established companies because they usually only have to address one thing at a time, stay on track and then just charge ahead. So let's stick to the principle of reverse engineering, but look at how a large well-established company has challenged its own core by using the same 'back to the present' method, and how it has driven the process through the creation of an X division that lays its strategies based on science fiction.

SCIENCE FICTION STRATEGIES

Meet Kyle Nel, one of the most radical innovators I've ever had the pleasure of knowing. In 2012, Kyle, a behavioural scientist, was asked to start Lowe's Innovation Labs.[10] If you're not familiar with Lowe's,[11] it's an American Fortune 40 company, a DIY chain, founded in 1946, with an annual revenue of almost $70 billion and more than 300,000 employees.[12] In other words, it's a giant and, in Kyle's own words, it's like most other boring traditional companies. That's why he wanted to work for them. His goal was to explore how to transform a large, old, traditional, dusty organization into one of the most innovative companies in the world. The hypothesis was that if you can transform Lowe's, you can transform anyone. A mission which succeeded when Lowe's was recognized as one of the most innovative companies in augmented and virtual reality by the leading technology medium Fast Company in 2018[13] and featured as one of the most admired companies in the world by business magazine Fortune Magazine.[14] These accolades were very far from Lowe's reality in 2012, when Kyle commenced his mission.

However, the success of the project is not only reflected in these acknowledgements, but in the specific forward-looking solutions that the company has developed. This applies, for example, to robot skeletons that shop workers can wear, also called exoskeletons, which gives them more power and ensures that they don't sustain wear-and-tear injuries; robot assistants which guide customers around the stores, speak multiple languages and scan shelves that need to be restocked; and the world's first 3D printer that is able to print in zero gravity and is currently printing tools for astronauts on the International Space Station. The method for succeeding was the creation of Lowe's Innovation Labs, an independent entity funded by the parent company, but operating independently of the headquarters. Lowe's Innovation Labs distinguishes itself further by working with a method that they call narrative-driven innovation, where you work your way back to today's solutions by developing science fiction scenarios to inspire the company's strategy work.

The method is described in detail by Kyle Nel and his co-authors, Professor of Neuroscience Thomas Ramsøy and INSEAD Professor Nathan Furr, in their book *Leading Transformation*,[15] and I have had the opportunity to follow this fascinating development close up. The starting point for their method leads us back to the same principles that we discussed in Chapter 2, 'What Is the Purpose?' People are driven by stories. The stories we tell each other enable us to understand each other's motives and to sense potential based on things beyond purely rational parameters. This recognition proves to be crucial in innovation contexts, even when it comes to convincing senior management about the strategies they need to lay or what projects to finance.

If you are in senior management at a large company, you have probably seen most things. A sea of consultants have been brought into the company to prepare analyses and propose strategies, numerous development projects have been launched, and an infinite number of buzzwords have been explored for their potential benefits. There's a good chance you've developed a well-trained bullshit detector (excuse the language) and a certain kind of cynicism that leads to the desire to see money before believing in the potential of a given project. 'Show me the money', as Cuba Gooding Jr said to Tom Cruise in the movie *Jerry Maguire*.[16]

In other words, in order to motivate senior management to conduct radical experiments and challenge the core organization that they work so hard to protect, you need to have a compelling story, and to not simply present the usual arguments in the usual ways. This is why Lowe's Innovation Labs began to produce science fiction comics for their senior management. Professional science fiction writers were given market and megatrend analyses from Lowe's analysis departments, and asked to use this data to develop scenarios that illustrated how Lowe's customers' lives could look ten years into the future. Professional science fiction writers were hired to ensure that they wouldn't just get traditional PowerPoint presentations back, but the development of narratives with protagonists, dilemmas, and solutions, the way we see them in novels and movies. These effects make the scenarios much more engaging, easier to identify with and, therefore, more difficult to maintain one's usual barriers against. Even for senior management. Finally, the stories were conveyed in comic book format, using the power of visualizing possible solutions, in order to surprise senior management with the alternative format. In this context, senior management could give input to the areas of action to be pursued, which Lowe's Innovation Labs could then develop prototypes for.

These prototypes were continuously tested on users using observations, eye tracking, and EEG studies.[17] EEG studies are performed by attaching electrodes on the respondents' heads to measure electrical impulses in the brain[18] and to, for example, reveal emotional involvement and cognitive load – i.e. if the brain is overwhelmed by information and therefore shuts down to receiving the messages – based on which brain areas are activated.[19] This approach gave the people from Lowe's Innovation Labs the opportunity to quickly learn what worked and what didn't work. It wouldn't have been possible to reveal these findings using regular survey techniques because a person's reactions happen unconsciously and therefore, per definition, can't be relayed by the individual respondent. At the same time, the human brain is such that if it doesn't know the answer to a question, it will just make it up. It's the classic, under-recognized problem with market analyses that causes people to not do what they say they will do. By using EEG, you can generate far more valid analysis results.

The method was successful and led to Kyle and his team getting funds to develop virtual and augmented reality rooms in a number of Lowe's DIY stores to experiment with the possibility that customers could enter these spaces, use the technology to insert Lowe's products into their own virtual homes, and, hence, make better purchasing decisions. Here, they used the developed future scenarios in which the science fiction authors imagined that augmented and virtual reality would be integral parts of human everyday tools in ten years' time. Then, the scenario was brought back into the present to identify the first products and processes that could be developed, to learn from the experiments and identify the business potentials. It's worth noting that this happened before the augmented reality game Pokémon Go, and Facebook's acquisition of virtual reality producer Oculus Rift that developed the first widely available virtual reality glasses, at a time when it wasn't obvious that augmented or virtual reality would become mainstream products.

My favourite example of how radically Lowe's Innovation Labs operated can be found in their work with 3D printing. An area that the science fiction writers continually returned to in their stories, and that Lowe's therefore decided to explore further – a possible future where you could print your products rather than buy them ready-made in a store. But where do you even begin, when faced with such a task? What is the first step? For Kyle and his team, the best first step turned out to be finding the right partners who could help them on their way, because they would possess technological skills that the organization did not have. It also turned out that the right partners would be what Kyle calls 'uncommon partners'. Instead of co-operating with large established players, who were often more interested in selling their existing solutions than developing shared experiments, Lowe's therefore looked for individuals and startups in other environments. In connection with the 3D print project, Lowe's found its uncommon partner at the educational institution Singularity University,[20] in one of their incubator's startups called Made in Space.[21]

Made in Space worked to develop 3D printers that can print in zero gravity, a not insignificant challenge, but a challenge that needed to be solved to realize the dream of making humanity interplanetary and making it possible to inhabit other planets. The alternative is to transport all building materials from the Earth into space, which is simultaneously impractical, expensive, and slow. If it was instead possible to print tools, spare parts, or building blocks on site, you could save a lot of time and money. The teams from Lowe's Innovation Labs and Made in Space sat together and used Lowe's science fiction comic about 3D printing of the future to jointly formulate a vision and, based on this, reverse engineer a design strategy to achieve that goal. The results speak for themselves. Today, as a consequence of the collaboration, the ISS has a 3D printer that prints tools on-site, which has reduced the cost of getting a new adjustable wrench delivered to the space station from many thousands of dollars (the cost of flying a bottle of water to the space station with a space rocket was somewhere between 9,000 and 43,000 dollars in 2016[22]) to just over seven dollars.

You could ask yourself why Lowe's, a large, old-fashioned DIY chain, decided to spend time and money developing a 3D printer that works in space, besides the fact that space is, of course, the next trillion-dollar market. The answer is that while developing 3D printers for space, experiences were gained that enabled the lab to develop 3D services for Lowe's own stores, allowing customers to print personalized solutions which hadn't been possible before. And, more importantly, the fact that Lowe's began experimenting with 3D print technologies several years before its relevance became evident to other actors means that Lowe's is now North America's leading expert in 3D printing in the retail industry. All of their competitors have to come to them to learn what to do, and all the data that Lowe's is now harvesting are valuable ingredients in the cocktail that might end up mutating Lowe's from the DIY chain they are today, to the data business they need to become 5, 10, 15 years into the future, if they are to maintain their relevance.

X DIVISIONS

Lowe's Innovation Labs' offices are located in a different American state from Lowe's. This was a conscious choice, as they knew from the very beginning that the projects that Lowe's Innovation Labs wanted to launch required other people, capabilities, and technologies than the company was used to. At the same time, the task was to carry out experiments that they didn't know would be successful and for which business cases hadn't been developed before starting. In other words, they used methods that were very different from those that the parent company was used to. By establishing the lab outside the headquarters, like an X division, the likelihood of success was optimized because the lab was given the opportunity to carry out its experiments without being surrounded by a parent company that constantly questioned its methods and results. At the same time, noise and uncertainty in the parent company were avoided, by not installing the lab and its strange projects in the midst of daily operations. However, an office at the headquarters has also been established, at a later point, which serves as a link between the lab's innovations and the parent organization, when the projects are ready for that move.

X divisions are not a new thing, but their proliferation has been accelerating sharply in recent years. The very first documented X division, called Skunk Works, was started by Lockheed Martin in 1943,[23] and achieved its first success by developing the Lockheed P-8+ Shooting Star plane's design in just 143 days in a secret laboratory away from the core company. Today, we are seeing more and more established organizations create similar units, which, however, vary significantly in size and design. Emerson, which develops climate technology, among other things, has a 40,000-square-foot test laboratory at the University of Dayton, where they have established test environments for private homes, a supermarket, a commercial kitchen, and a data centre to prototype new services.[24] Caterpillar has students and their own employees at an innovation lab at the University of Illinois to develop new data-driven projects that are meant to grow big enough to become independent business units and to use capabilities and technologies beyond those than the organization currently utilizes in its core company.[25] Amazon established their Lab 126 in Silicon Valley, away from the Seattle headquarters, when they developed Kindle in the mid-2000s. Today, the laboratory has 3000 employees.[26] A few years ago, IKEA established Space10 in Copenhagen, as a future living lab, to explore new opportunities for creating better, more sustainable living conditions,[27] possibilities that are not currently part of the core company.

The logistics giant Maersk has also established their version of an X division called Maersk Growth, which operates as a venture arm from its own offices at Christianshavn, Copenhagen, away from the legendary headquarters on the Esplanade. The unit was founded to develop Maersk's adjacencies, i.e. potential business areas, away from the core, and their task is to focus on investments and building new businesses. In addition, the unit has another interesting mandate, which is to use its learnings to strengthen the entire organization's entrepreneurship capabilities. The man hired to realize these ambitions is Sune Stilling, a veteran of both the oil and logistics world. He was assigned to help Maersk into the future by experimenting with and exploring the areas that are not the core capabilities of the organization. The unit's focus areas were revealed through strategy work, which looked at megatrends and their expected impact on the world in 2030–2050 to identify the biggest long-term potentials. This revelation manifested itself in three concrete, yet broadly defined domains, which are about creating next-generation logistics, improving global trade opportunities, and combating food waste.

The ambitions are big. It is about developing independent business legs that may be relocated back to the core company when the time is ripe, or which may remain independent entities, and which are not expected to earn money for the organization until three to seven years down the line, with a high risk of failure. The idea is that this self-contained Growth unit can get resources, special data, customers, and testing opportunities from the parent company while allowing the unit to operate with the agility of a startup and, not least, to set up systems for the parent organization's entrepreneurial initiatives.

It turned out that, when Sune and his team carried out their initial analyses, there was a sea of different entrepreneurship projects in the Maersk organization. They found a total of 41 different initiatives covering everything from mobile internet in Africa to new fuel types and autonomous ships. These were all exciting and potentially valuable projects, but all the work was without structure, driven by individuals' energy and entrepreneurial spirits, without a strategic support system to support development, and without specific measurement points and success parameters. This meant that projects could suddenly lose their funding or crew because there were other needs in the organization, or because individuals got new jobs and left the company.

At the same time, the Growth team spotted valuable projects that didn't get the attention and funding they needed, including a partnership with IBM to develop an open logistics platform using blockchain technology. The team got this project upgraded so that it could be launched as an independent company, TradeLens,[28] in August 2018. The purpose of TradeLens is to build a digital platform where all players, including Maersk's competitors, can conduct safer and more transparent trade and exchange of data. The purpose of using blockchain technology is that you can use so-called smart contracts, i.e. digital contracts in a database that nobody can manipulate, and you can make data exchange much faster and less error-prone. One test run of the platform showed reduced transportation time of material by 40%, which saved the parties involved thousands of dollars. If it is possible to scale this project, billions in savings could potentially go to the logistics industry.[29]

The development and acceleration of the TradeLens project would never have been possible in Maersk's core business as the project is far too distant from the day-to-day operations and organization's existing focus. It wouldn't have been possible for the core company to give the project sufficient focus, which was also what the Growth team's analyses proved was the case. By taking the project out of the core company and giving it the attention of the Growth unit, the project owners could focus wholeheartedly on the project's needs. Maersk and IBM are not the only actors working to develop these kinds of platforms, so the competition is great, but if they succeed in making the project a success and gaining critical mass, they have a potential game changer on their hands. Perhaps even with such great potential that TradeLens could become a decisive driving force in the necessary mutation of Maersk's future business.

Like Lowe's, which opened its innovation lab with one man (today, they are 200-strong), Maersk Growth also started small. In the initial long period of time, Sune and one part-time worker were the ones who built the unit. Now they are 20 people, and they are still growing. And a careful expansion is smart, because just as X divisions like Maersk Growth and Lowe's Innovation Labs are conducting experiments, they are, to begin with, experiments in and of themselves which need to find the right form and focus. Maersk Growth initially served the purpose of building companies from scratch, but this proved extremely difficult because it required its few employees to generate the right ideas themselves, qualify these ideas, put together the right team that was motivated enough to work on the projects as corporate founders, and work on scaling them. Therefore, Growth ended up pivoting, as it is called in the world of entrepreneurship, which means that they changed strategy, and decided to focus 90% of their energy on investment and only 10% on building projects from scratch. The advantage is that it's much faster and less resource-consuming to find the right startups that are already in progress and have identified the relevant ideas and strong teams to further develop the projects. An advantage that we also discovered when discussing the advantages of establishing collaborations with external accelerators. Another discovery that Maersk Growth made was that it is necessary to define the right purpose of your initiatives. Originally, Maersk Growth's initial purpose was to create 'billion-dollar businesses', but soon they found that it was far more motivating for people to go to work to fight food waste than to create billionaires, so this experience was crucial to the unit's focus and communication. These kinds of learnings are much easier to respond to when there are only a handful of people than when you are a large well-established organization with established routines. Therefore, you should always begin your experiments on a small scale.

X divisions are important tools for developing future business areas so that they may mutate the core of major established organizations over time. It is clear that partnerships are crucial to this success, including: those between established organizations, such as Maersk's cooperation with IBM; those between established organizations and universities such as Caterpillar and Emerson; and those between established organizations and startups, such as Lowe's collaboration with various entrepreneurs. There are also ample opportunities to establish partnerships with larger ecosystems. For example, collaborations with accelerators and incubators, as we have previously discussed, could be the ones to provide access to the most interesting startups. But this could also happen through collaborations with innovation platforms. One of the most interesting partnerships at a global level here is the collaboration between Japan's leading airline ANA and the open innovation platform XPRIZE, which are currently running an exciting radical experiment.

RADICAL OPEN INNOVATION

The Japanese population is expected to fall from 128 million in 2008 to only 88 million by 2050.[30] For a company like the Japanese airline All Nippon Airways (ANA), which has traditionally focused on the domestic market and doesn't have a strong international brand, you could see from a mile away that this is a disaster, even though it is the country's leading airline. Therefore, ANA laid a globalization strategy that was first and foremost carried by marketing.

In 2015, Jun Suto, the founder and CEO of the company s-cubed consulting with more than 25 years of global experience, started working with the XPRIZE Foundation. XPRIZE is a non-profit organization that aims to create global open innovation competitions that try to solve the world's biggest problems. The very first competition was completed between 1996 and 2004, in which the challenge was to build a manned spacecraft that could fly into the stratosphere twice within two weeks. Hundreds of global teams tried to solve this problem. The winning team won 10 million dollars and was purchased by Richard Branson, who established Virgin Galactic from the project, which was the actual beginning of commercial space travel.

Today, there are a number of XPRIZEs, including a Global Learning XPRIZE with the purpose of developing open source scalable software that allows children around the world to teach themselves how to read, write, and calculate;[31] an Ocean Discovery XPRIZE[32] with the purpose of developing technology that can operate at enormous depths and explore the oceans; and a Lunar XPRIZE,[33] which aims to develop technology that enables private organizations to fly to the Moon. Jun was the man who got ANA on board as a sponsor in connection with the Lunar XPRIZE Global Summit in Tokyo, which was ANA's first involvement with XPRIZE. Before 2016, XPRIZE developed its own competitions internally, but they subsequently decided to open the design process so that outside companies could compete about the problems to be solved. Meanwhile, Jun had become the XPRIZE Visioneers Prize Developer, i.e. one of the people who helps companies develop their competition concepts. Together with the scientist Dr. Harry Kllon, PhD Perdue, Akira Fukabori, and Kevin Kajitani, ANA Avatar co-directors and two other competition developers (Ioan Istrate and MacKenzie Richter), his team developed ANA's involvement from being purely brand-oriented to influencing the innovation agenda itself.

At the time, ANA had developed a vision to connect all the world's 7.5 billion people with each other, and since only about 6% of the world's population has travelled by air,[34] it became evident that they needed to think along different lines and utilize new technological opportunities to a greater extent. Together with a number of other external companies and teams, ANA pitched its competitive ideas to XPRIZE and were victorious. This resulted in the creation of the ANA Avatar XPRIZE competition.[35]

While reading about this vision of connecting all the world's 7.5 billion people using technology and developing long-distance travel methods, you were probably thinking that ANA should develop a teleporter, like the one from Star Trek. 'Scotty, Beam me up', as Captain Kirk famously said to his chief engineer Montgomery Scott[36] every time he needed to be teleported from some exotic planet out in the infinite space back to the Starship Enterprise. (If you weren't thinking along those lines, I apologize for the nerdiness, which must obviously have been incomprehensible.) And the ANA team thought along those lines as well. They asked themselves: 'What is the ultimate transport possibility?' which led them to teleportation and a search for how they could contribute to the development of the field.

The ANA team described their ambition to create 'unlimited travel by teleporting your consciousness into a physical avatar body that enables people to instantly be in multiple places at once'.[37] The project extends over four years with several inbuilt milestones, where the teams that are accepted as participants must continuously prove how far they've come and qualify to move on to the next rounds. The first prototypes use different versions of virtual reality glasses to ensure that the user can see; gloves with haptics that help them hold and feel objects across distances; and physical robots at the other end that the user can manipulate using these tools. We have to wait until April 2022 to find out what the final winning solution looks like.

Overall, ANA has committed itself to spending $22 million on the project.[38] But that is small change, when you think about the hundreds of millions of dollars of value that the many enrolled teams' research and development brings back to ANA, as well as the branding value that the company gains for running the competition. And ANA couldn't hire the teams working to solve the task even if they wanted to, because the teams that sign up for the competition don't do it because they want to work for a big airline company, but because they think it's an exciting problem that they want to solve.

The application possibilities of an avatar are many. The XPRIZE organization considers the most immediate ones to be disaster relief in places where people can't be sent in and when there is a need for critical repairs that could only be carried out by very few highly specialized people. But other obvious opportunities for use also include being able to 'teleport' yourself to foreign destinations and be with family and friends in even more vivid ways than are currently possible with today's technology, even if you've become too old for long journeys or you have physical disabilities.

ANA's journey with XPRIZE began as a branding project funded by the marketing department, but the ambition level evolved as quickly as the organization saw the potential in the results that could be achieved. In 2016, ANA also opened a digital design lab, where the Avatar project is located. The lab is legally a part of the parent group ANA Holdings, but doesn't have direct reporting obligations to the airline. The Avatar project was placed in the design lab because the work they do there is radically different from anything else that is done in the organization; hence, there is a need for capabilities, technologies, and collaborations that are completely different from those which are traditionally used.

And the ambitions don't stop here. The latest step, taken in September 2018, was to establish Avatar X,[39] a consortium that includes collaborations with JAXA (Japan Aerospace Exploration Agency), because perhaps the greatest potential lies in creating avatar solutions for the parts of the universe that are hardest to access, and where it makes the least sense to send people. If ANA succeeds with its Avatar project, this radical open innovation project will have been the catalyst for mutating the core of the organization to realize the vision of connecting all the world's 7.5 billion people – throughout space.

NEW ORGANIZATIONS

In 2015, Google was renamed Alphabet. In connection to this, the company was reorganized and the Google part of the business, consisting of search and advertising, which generate the vast majority of the organization's revenue and earnings, was separated from all other activity. All the other activity is also called 'other bets'. Other bets include Verily,[40] which performs basic research in the field of disease prevention; Sidewalk Labs,[41] which works to develop intelligent cities; Calico,[42] aimed at radically increasing people's lifespans; DeepMind,[43] which conducts research in artificial intelligence and became known for developing Google DeepMind, the artificial intelligence that beat the world's best Go player; Google Ventures, or GV,[44] Alphabet's investment company with billions to invest in new companies; and X,[45] the organization's 'moonshot factory', which aims to invent the future. The reason for splitting up into the new units was to give the Google part, the traditional part of the organization, more peace to focus solely on its core business, thus giving its investors more peace of mind about the many side activities which, so far, haven't generated any earnings for the company, and which may seem like noise to an investor. At the same time, the separation meant that the other individual initiatives were more able to stand on their own two feet and become further developed as independent businesses with the risks that this entails. If they fail, they must die, as there is no longer a rich parent organization that can simply finance the deficit.

The moonshot factory X, which is managed day-to-day by Astro Teller (it's a bought name. I've researched it) who is famous for always having a pair of roller skates on so he can get around quickly, is tasked with exploring and developing radical ideas that could potentially transform the world. One of the methods used to determine which projects to put in motion is the simple question: 'Can we imagine a future that doesn't involve x' where 'x' could be anything. If the X team's answer to this question is 'No, we can't imagine it' or 'We don't know', then there is good reason to do some preliminary investigations.

The question has, among other things, resulted in the fact that X was one of the first to begin developing self-driving cars and augmented reality glasses, Google Glass. The glasses were not a hit, although they have started being used again in the health-care sector. But since X is a laboratory for radical experiments, most developments are expected to fail. On the other hand, the self-driving cars turned out to be so viable, that the unit has been separated out and made into an independent company, Waymo.[46] And that's X's strategy. If experiments prove viable, they are separated from the moonshot factory and are to stand on their own feet. In X, this is referred to as the projects graduating, just like college students. When projects graduate, they must also move away from home, earn their own money, and pay their own bills. However, this also means that until projects have graduated from X, no attention is paid to business models and expected financial results, which is generally a classic mistake that many companies make with their experiments. They expect developed business models and proof of projects' financial sustainability much too early on. But if you have very big ambitions for your experiments, such as developing self-driving cars, then the incubation period is long, and expectations of rapid economic results can be directly dangerous to projects' potential at this stage, because it increases focus on short-term gains over long-term potential.

X's most recent graduated projects are called Loon and Wing.[47] The Loon project develops air balloons, which can be sent all the way up to the stratosphere, and transmit WiFi to strategically positioned receivers from there, so that sparsely populated parts of the world can get online as well. So far, the project has flown almost 30 million kilometres and, among other things, demonstrated its effect when the balloons were used in Puerto Rico after Hurricane Maria that destroyed the island's infrastructure in 2018. The Loon balloons were the direct reasons why both dispersed families and emergency people could communicate.

The second project, Wing, builds drones. The drones became particularly famous when they managed to deliver pizzas to hungry Australians. But although it's fun, smart, and useful, the team weren't really sure that the drones' success justified making Wing its own company. Project managers were first reassured when they decided to make the project challenge harder, and to make the problem bigger. It's one thing to be able to deliver things with drones – there are many companies working to make that possible. But who or what will make sure that there are safeguards for all the many drones that want to use the airspace to deliver pizzas and other things? That matter was unclear. What was clear, however, was that if no one developed the system that could control all the many future drones, then the consequence would be that the world's governments would legislate against them. Therefore, Wing decided not only to develop drones, but to develop an air control system that can control drones and help them navigate through the airspace in an appropriate and safe way. It was this decision that finally convinced the X management team in charge of deciding Wings's destiny that there was also a business model in the project that was strong enough for them to let it graduate and become its own independent company, where the hope is that the company can grow big and strong.

Toyota has also founded a new independent company. It is called Toyota Research Institute-Advanced Development (TRI-AD) and, so far, it has received $2.8 billion in capital.[48] The new company also needs a lot of money to help Toyota realize the ambition of testing their electric self-driving cars by 2020 by developing the software. In this context, the most interesting thing, however, is the fact that Toyota has decided to establish

TRI-AD as an independent company. A sprout of the existing Toyota Research Institute. Management has estimated that they are more likely to achieve their ambitions this way, rather than establishing a unit internally within the existing organization, mainly due to the need for recruitment of the right capabilities and the desire to establish the right culture. To begin with, 300 people have been recruited for the new organization, but this number is meant to increase to 1000 within a short period of time. According to statements from a Toyota spokesperson for the *Wall Street Journal*, there is a need for a global team and 'one of the best ways to do that is to create a company separate from Toyota Motor Corp., to create a company with different rules – like a startup'.[49]

If you look at the general development of self-driving cars, virtually all major car manufacturers are setting up independent entities to develop their capabilities in the field of transport, as are many of the new players entering the markets that traditionally belonged to carmakers. Ford has recently announced the establishment of Ford Smart Mobility, a unit headquartered in Silicon Valley, to develop new business areas such as car sharing and parking apps.[50] GM (General Motors) has purchased the self-driving car company Cruise Automation to develop their capabilities in the relevant technologies.[51] TomTom, especially known for their GPSs, has recently bought the Berlin-based self-driving automotive software company Autonomous.[52]

Blackberry, which is best known for its smartphone of the same name, and which has been struggling for many years, is on its way with a self-driving car research centre that is being set up outside its headquarters by expanding an existing subsidiary.[53] The microchip manufacturer Intel recently bought the self-driving car company Mobileye for more than $15 billion.[54] And I could go on and on.

What this development also shows is that one of the fastest ways to mutate an organization and explore radically new business areas that potentially challenge the company's existing core is through acquisitions, and secondly through investments that may end up in acquisition. That is also why the creation of investment companies is one of the most frequently used tools among large companies. In this field, we see organizations like Tyson, the world's largest meat producer, investing in, among others, Beyond Meat, which manufactures plant-based products that simulate the meat-eating experience;[55] IKEA collaborating with Olafur Eliasson's Little Sun project that aims to create solar-powered products for parts of the world which don't have access to electricity;[56] or Microsoft that first invested in, and subsequently purchased, LinkedIn. According to Microsoft CEO Satya Nadella, investments are often the best strategy for making successful acquisitions because it is a more secure method of first getting to know the new organizations and thoroughly exploring the synergies between the two units.[57]

However, it requires some degree of patience and, as we have seen in the development of self-driving cars, the players are under significant time pressure, which is causing them to throw a lot of money at acquisitions and the creation of new units.

Buying and establishing new businesses is one way to do it. However, the creation of X divisions, innovation labs and radical open innovation projects where you can, among other things, use narrative driven strategies to work back to the present from your highly ambitious visions, can be extremely valuable methods for future-proofing your organization. It will be exciting to see who succeeds in creating successful mutations of their existing core companies using these methods.

NOTES

1. www.biography.com/news/arthur_c_clarke_biography_facts.
2. https://quoteinvestigator.com/2017/06/09/elevator.
3. https://theculturetrip.com/north-america/usa/articles/10-inventions-no-one-thought-would-be-a-success.
4. www.sciencealert.com/japan-testing-space-elevator-scale-model-shizuoka-university.
5. www.obayashi.co.jp/en/special/skytree.html.
6. www.gaia.com/article/japan-space-elevator.
7. www.scmp.com/news/china/society/article/2170193/china-has-strongest-fibre-can-haul-160-elephants-and-space.
8. PwC 2017 Global Digital IQ Survey.
9. www.ispace-inc.com.
10. www.lowesinnovationlabs.com.
11. www.lowes.com.

12. https://en.wikipedia.org/wiki/Lowe%27s.
13. www.fastcompany.com/company/lowes.
14. http://archive.fortune.com/magazines/fortune/most-admired/2012/top358/L.html.
15. Nathan Furr, Kyle Nel & Thomas Zoega Ramsøy: Leading Transformation: How to Take Charge of Your Company's Future, 2018.
16. www.youtube.com/watch?v=mBS0OWGUidc.
17. Abbreviation for ElectroEncephaloGram.
18. https://en.wikipedia.org/wiki/Electroencephalography.
19. www.neuronsinc.com.
20. www.su.org.
21. http://madeinspace.us.
22. www.businessinsider.com/spacex-rocket-cargo-price-by-weight-2016-6?r=US&IR=T&IR=T.
23. https://en.wikipedia.org/wiki/Skunk_Works.
24. https://climate.emerson.com/en-us/tools-resources/the-helix.
25. https://www.caterpillar.com/en/company/innovation/customer-solutions/data-analytics/innovation-lab.html.
26. https://amazon.jobs/en/teams/lab126.
27. https://space10.io/.
28. https://www.tradelens.com/.
29. https://newsroom.ibm.com/2018-08-09-Maersk-and-IBM-Introduce-TradeLens-Blockchain-Shipping-Solution.
30. www.japantimes.co.jp/news/2017/04/10/national/social-issues/japans-population-projected-plunge-88-million-2065/#.W9Wez3ozb_8.
31. www.xprize.org/prizes/global-learning.
32. https://oceandiscovery.xprize.org/prizes/ocean-discovery.
33. https://lunar.xprize.org/prizes/lunar.
34. https://hiptokyo.jp/hiptalk/innovation_ana.
35. www.xprize.org/prizes/avatar.
36. www.youtube.com/watch?v=west2PFD0D4.
37. www.businesswire.com/news/home/20160816005401/en/XPRIZE-Launches-New-Visioneering-Model-Evaluating-Selecting.

38. https://medium.com/abundance-insights/avatars-future-of-transportation-a99128712e92.
39. http://global.jaxa.jp/press/2018/09/20180906_avatarx.html.
40. https://verily.com.
41. www.sidewalklabs.com.
42. www.calicolabs.com.
43. https://deepmind.com.
44. www.gv.com.
45. https://x.company.
46. https://waymo.com.
47. www.wired.com/story/alphabet-google-x-innovation-loon-wing-graduation.
48. https://futurism.com/toyota-self-driving-car-company.
49. www.wsj.com/articles/toyota-announces-new-company-devoted-to-self-driving-cars-1519976923.
50. https://hbr.org/2016/12/when-large-companies-are-better-at-entrepreneurship-than-startups.
51. www.techworld.com/picture-gallery/data/-companies-working-on-driverless-cars-3641537.
52. https://www.businessinsider.com/tomtom-acquired-autonomous-berlin-based-autonomous-driving-startup-as-it-gears-up-for-the-future-2017-1?r=US&IR=T.
53. https://venturebeat.com/2016/12/18/blackberry-to-open-autonomous-vehicle-hub/.
54. https://www.businessinsider.com/intel-mobileye-acquisition-report-2017-3?r=US&IR=T&IR=T.
55. https://techcrunch.com/2018/05/02/tyson-foods-investment-arm-backs-another-lab-grown-meat-manufacturer/.
56. https://littlesun.com/littlesunikea/.
57. Satya Nadella, Hit Refresh, 2017.

CONCLUSION

Innovation is no longer a function that belongs to a special department down in the company's basement. Innovation has to be embedded in every company's DNA and all employees are important parts of the innovation team. This recognition is spreading to more and more companies and it is crucial to their long-term success.

At the same time, company executives need to understand and acknowledge that innovation is not a homogeneous thing, but that innovation must be carried out in different ways depending on what the goal is. As I've described in detail in the third part of the book, there are fundamental differences between whether you are upgrading the core of your organization through augmenting innovation, or challenging the core through mutating innovation. It requires different people, capabilities and even different physical entities. And it requires a sustained, targeted, and dedicated focus on people. You can only succeed by transforming your organizational culture to foster innovation. This might be where the biggest challenges lie: To create a true innovation culture that challenges the status quo in a constructive way, where employees are comfortable with continuous change, by addressing the barriers that the individual, organizational, and societal immune systems represent, as discussed in Part Two.

To even reach that point, where you can create successful innovations, you need to sharpen the axe, and many fail to fully understand that, as the world changes, so do the answers to the important questions. It is no longer easy to answer the question of which industry you are in, or even who your competitors are. But if you explore the questions deeply enough and you push your own limits, you will enter entirely new opportunity spaces.

Technological achievements create unprecedented opportunities and challenge the core of any organization. No matter what product, service, or experience you create, you can't rest on your laurels. You have to bring yourself to a position where you have a clear strategy for both optimizing, augmenting, and mutating your core and thus transform your legacy organization.

It's not an easy job. But, hey, if it were easy, everyone would be doing it. Those who make it, on the other hand, will be the innovation champions of the future.

BIBLIOGRAPHY

Banbury, S. and D, Berry. (1998) 'Disruption of office-related tasks by speech and office noise.' *British Journal of Psychology*, 89 (3), pp. 499–517. ISSN 0007-1269.

Brandt, Anthony A. and David Eagleman. (2017) *The Runaway Species: How Human Creativity Remakes the World*. Catapult.

Cirillo, Francesco (2018) *The Pomodoro Technique: The Life-Changing Time Management System*. Virgin Books.

Day, George S. (2003) 'Is it Real? Can We Win? Is It Worth Doing?' *HBR, On Innovation*. Harvard Business Review Press.

Diamandis, Peter and Steven Kotler (2015) *Bold: How to Go Big, Create Wealth and Impact the World*. Simon & Schuster.

Doerr, John (2018) *Measure What Matters: OKRs – The Simple Idea That Drives 10x Growth*. Penguin.

Doudna, Jennifer (2018) *A Crack in Creation: The New Power to Control Evolution*. Vintage.

Eagleman, David (2015) *The Brain: The Story of You*. Canongate Books.

Edmondson, Amy (1999) 'Psychological Safety and Learning Behavior in Work Teams', *Administrative Science Quarterly*, Vol. 44, No. 2 (Jun., 1999), pp. 350–383.

Erixon Fredrik and Björn Weigel (2016) *The Innovation Illusion: How So Little is Created by So Many Working So Hard*. Yale University Press.

Florida, Richard (2011) *The Great Reset: How New Ways of Living and Working Drive Post-Crash Prosperity*. Harper Business.

Frey, Bruno S. and Margit Osterloh (2002) *Successful Management by Motivation*. Springer.

Furr, Nathan, Kyle Nell and Thomas Zoëga Ramsøy (2018) *Leading Transformation: How to Take Charge of Your Company's Future*. Harvard Business Review Press.

Galloway, Scott (2017) *The Four: The Hidden DNA of Amazon, Apple, Facebook and Google*. Penguin.

Gittell, J. Hoffer (1999) *Anomalies of High Performance: Reframing Economic and Organizational Theory of Performance Management*. Harvard University Press.

Goffman, Erving (1974) *Frame Analysis: An Essay on the Organization of Experience.* Northeastern University Press.

Green, Joshua (2013) *Moral Tribes: Emotion, Reason and the Gap Between Us and Them.* Atlantic Books.

Ismail, Salim, Yuri van Geest and Michael S. Malone (2014) *Exponential Organizations: Why New Organizations are Ten Times Better, Faster and Cheaper Than Yours (and What To Do About It).* Diversion Publishing.

Juma, Calestous (2016) *Innovation and its Enemies: Why People Resist New Technologies.* Oxford University Press.

Kahneman, Daniel (2012) *Thinking Fast and Slow.* Penguin.

Kim, Gene, Jez Humble, Patrick Debois and John Willis (2016) *The DevOps Handbook: How to Create World-Class Agility, Reliability & Security in Technology Organizations.* IT Revolution Press.

Knott, Anne Marie (2017) *How Innovation Really Works: Using the Trillion-Dollar R&D Fix to Drive Growth.* McGraw Hill Education.

Kotler, Steven (2014) *The Rise of Superman: Decoding the Science of Ultimate Human Performance.* Quercus Publishing.

Kotler, Steven and Jamie Wheal (2017) *Stealing Fire: How Silicon Valley, the Navy SEALs, and Maverick Scientists are Revolutionizing the Way We Live and Work.* Harper Collins.

Lewis, Michael (2017)*The Undoing Project: A Friendship that Changed the World.* Penguin.

Muller, Jerry Z (2017) *The Tyranny of Metrics.* Princeton University Press.

Nadella, Satya (2017) *Hit Refresh: The Quest to Rediscover Microsoft's Soul and Imagine a Better Future for Everyone.* William Collins.

Nørretranders, Tor (1999) *The User Illusion: Cutting Consciousness Down to Size.* Penguin.

Pawlak, Laila and Kris Østergaard (2016) *The Fundamental 4s: How to Design Extraordinary Customer Experiences in an Exponential World.* https://dare2.dk/fundamental-4s/.

Persson, Ingmar and Julian Savulescu (2012) *Unfit for the Future: The Need for Moral Enhancement.* Oxford University Press.

Poundstone, William (1999) *Prisoner's Dilemma.* Anchor Books.

Ries, Eric (2011) *The Lean Startup.* Crown Business.

Rossman, John (2016) *The Amazon Way on IoT: 10 Principles for Every Leader from the World's Leading Internet of Things Strategies.* Clyde Hill Publishing.

Schmidt, Eric (2015) *How Google Works.* John Murray.

Schumpeter, Joseph (2010) *Capitalism, Socialism and Democracy.* Routledge.

Schwab, Klaus (2017) *The Fourth Industrial Revolution.* Penguin.

Scott G., L.E. Leritz and M.D. Mumford (2004) 'The effectiveness of creativity training: A quantitative review.' *Creat. Res. J.* 16, pp. 361–388.

Simler, Kevin and Robin Hanson (2018) *The Elephant in the Brain: Hidden Motives in Everyday Life.* Oxford University Press.

Starek, Joanna E. and Caroline F. Keating (2010) 'Self-deception and its relationship to success in competition', *Basic and Applied Social Psychology*, Vol 12, Issue 2, pp. 145–155.

Stone, Brad (2014) *The Everything Store: Jeff Bezos and the Age of Amazon.* Corgi.

INDEX

repetition suppression 174
reverse engineering 217
reward systems 80, 81–9, 98, 121
Richter, MacKenzie 232
Ries, Eric: *Lean Startup, The* 142
Ringnes, Isabelle 183, 186, 187
risk profiles 67, 72
Rogers, Everett 113

Salesforce 89
  1-1-1 model 204
SAP 115, 116
Schmidt, Eric 81
Schumpeter 117, 119
science fiction strategies 217–24
scientific management theories 85
self-deception 24
self-driving cars 38, 39, 62–3, 64,
    96, 237, 239, 240
self-driving taxis 19
Serafeim, George 30
Shark Tank 157
#ShesGotThis 183
Shizuoka University 211
Sidewalk Labs 236
Silicon Valley 1, 15, 21, 114, 148,
    184, 240
Singularity University 199
  Global Startup Program 57, 151
SingularityU Nordic 167
'six degrees of competition' 58
'six degrees of separation' 59
skunk works 214
Slack 176
small and medium-sized enterprises
    (SMEs) 116, 118

'small world' problem 58, 59
smart contracts 228
Smart startups 55
social recognition 50
societal immune systems 8, 9, 98,
    101–22
Softbank 18, 95
solar energy111
Sopranos, The 94
South by South West 153
spillover effect 29
Spotify 1, 95
Stage Gate model 195
Star Trek 233
Starbucks 61, 63
Startupbootcamp 151
status quo bias 25, 31
Stenmann, Henrik 190
Stephens, Robert 127
Stilling, Sune 226–7
story, company 26, 27, 31
Sun Microsystems 173
'sunk-cost fallacy' 26, 87
Suto, Jun 231
SWAT team 115

Talya, Akanksha Manik 140
Tata: 'Dare to Try' prize 202
Taylor, Frederick 85
TDC 147
TechStars 57, 150
Telia 56
Tencent 18
TENK (Technology Network for
    Women) 183
Tesla 2, 27–8, 29, 44–5, 95, 96, 108